16,045

the ocean laboratory

CREATIVE SCIENCE SERIES

ETTA SCHNEIDER RESS, Ed.D., *editor-in-chief*

GERHARD RAMBERG, *art editor*   BUEFORD D. SMITH, *art editor*

PLANETS, STARS AND SPACE

JOSEPH MILES CHAMBERLAIN, Ed.D.
Assistant Director, The American
Museum of Natural History
KENNETH L. FRANKLIN, Ph.D.,
Astronomer, American Museum —
Hayden Planetarium
THOMAS D. NICHOLSON, Ph.D.,
Chairman and Astronomer,
American Museum — Hayden
Planetarium

THE EARTH'S STORY

GERALD AMES and ROSE WYLER
Authors, *The Golden Book of
Astronomy, The Story of the
Ice Age, The Golden Book of
Biology, Planet Earth, Food
and Life*

THE WAY OF THE WEATHER

JEROME SPAR, Ph.D., Professor
Department of Meteorology and
Oceanography
New York University, N.Y.

ATOMS, ENERGY AND MACHINES

JACK MCCORMICK, Ph.D., Curator
The Academy of Natural Sciences
of Philadelphia, Pennsylvania

The four books above are also available in Spanish.

THE LIVES OF ANIMALS

SYDNEY ANDERSON, Ph.D., Associate
Curator, American Museum of
Natural History, New York

MAN FROM THE BEGINNING

STANLEY A. FREED, Ph.D., Associate
Curator, American Museum of
Natural History, New York
RUTH S. FREED, Ph.D., Assistant
Professor of Anthropology, New
York University, New York

THE OCEAN LABORATORY

ATHELSTAN SPILHAUS, D.Sc.
Formerly Dean, Institute of
Technology,
University of Minnesota

FOOD AND LIFE

GERALD AMES and ROSE WYLER
Authors, *The Golden Book of
Astronomy, The Story of the Ice
Age, The Golden Book of Biology,
Planet Earth, The Earth's Story*

2

the ocean laboratory

by

Athelstan Spilhaus

published by

CREATIVE EDUCATIONAL SOCIETY, INC.

Mankato, Minnesota

in co-operation with

THE AMERICAN MUSEUM OF NATURAL HISTORY

New York, New York

THE OCEAN LABORATORY

ACKNOWLEDGMENTS

For this book I have drawn on earlier manuscripts and speeches that I have made in the past years, among them *Turn to the Sea* published by the National Academy of Sciences; *The Future of the Oceans* published by the Smithsonian Institution; *The Concept of a Sea Grant College* published in the *Congressional Record; Exploitation of the Sea* in *Tomorrow's Wilderness* The Sierra Club, San Francisco; I have also used ideas from discussions with many colleagues at Woods Hole Oceanographic Institution, Scripps Institute of Oceanography, Rhode Island School of Oceanography, Marine Institute, University of Miami and others. To all of these sources I owe my thanks. My thanks also goes to Dr. Dale Chelberg for his help in organizing this material and to Bueford Smith for his design and illustration of the entire book.

ATHELSTAN SPILHAUS

CONTENTS

INTRODUCTION

Man's study of the oceans has been, from the beginning, an eminently practical occupation. He wanted to extend trade to other countries, to find new and quicker routes, and to acquire knowledge of tides, currents, waves and winds that would enable him to make quicker and safer passages. He also sought to use the food and material resources of the oceans to commercial advantage. Whatever he tried had a useful purpose—the engineering of the oceans.

However, in later years enlightened people realized the need for basic research. Soon the oceans were being investigated for no other purpose than to satisfy the curiosity of intelligent and observant minds. Though such research is not directly useful, it is science, the first step to an understanding of the world around us. And science has proven its worth to engineering, for it provides many of the discoveries on which engineering builds.

In the past few years there has been an explosive awakening of interest in the oceans. Athelstan Spilhaus is well qualified to write about the oceans since he was one of the first to bring their scientific and practical importance to the attention of the government and general public. His bathythermograph was the first of the new family of modern oceanographic instruments. He developed it before World War II, when we were mostly using equipment designed 50 to 100 years previously.

Dr. Spilhaus' *The Ocean Laboratory* is not merely a review of present-day advances in oceanography or of the even more exciting possibilities of the future. It describes in clear and stimulating language how scientific achievements are a foundation for engineering. It is a well balanced book and a welcome change from the flood of enthusiastic misinformation about our new ocean frontier which is presently clogging the bookstores. Above all, it is concise and relates the story of ocean research simply and effectively. To quote from Jonathan Richardson, "Fewer words would not have served the turn, and more would have been superfluous."

DR. F. G. WALTON SMITH
Director, Institute of Marine Science
University of Miami
Miami, Florida

Part One

THE EARTH AND SEA

EARTH — A LABORATORY OF THE UNIVERSE

Our universe has many parts, all of which are related. To understand our earth, sun, the other planets of our solar system and the space through which they move, we must treat them as a whole. The birth of the earth was part of the origin of our galaxy, and because the age of our earth is a sizable fraction of the age of the galaxy on whose fringe we ride, the study of the history of our planet is a laboratory study of the history of the universe. But three-quarters of our laboratory is under water! We live on land and know more about that part of the earth's surface than anything else, but the part under water has even more to show us.

This "inner space" on our planet, which is in many respects more important to us, more unknown and at least as interesting as outer space, is inundated by ocean waters which cover much of the record of history beneath them. They hide the shape of the sea floor; they make it difficult to go down and drill into that floor; and they cover fossil sediments, the layers of which are the pages of earth history even before life originated and evolved. At the same time, they preserve the layers which, on the land quarter, are often erased or jumbled by the continual processes of weathering by air, water and mountain building. The look and make-up of the ocean floor miles down give hints about what lies deeper and may extend to the very core of the earth. This huge volume

of water, the world ocean, we can neither see through without instruments nor explore without special vessels to carry us. Man has the ability to make these instruments and vessels and the oceans are now beginning to yield their secrets.

The experimental craft Aluminaut *puts out into a shimmering sea beneath a late afternoon sun.*

The earth's water space is vital to us in many ways. The ocean is the source of the water that enters the atmosphere and forms our clouds, falls on our continents, and returns by our rivers to the sea. It is the ocean which stores heat in the summer, liberates it in the winter, and exerts a profound effect on the tempering of climate. On the other hand, it is the winds in the atmosphere that stir up the waves and cause the surface currents of the ocean to flow. The ocean is the home of many living things, a big biological engine where tiny green plants take the sunlight in the top layers of the water and combine it with inorganic chemicals through photosynthesis. These phytoplankton, the grasses of the sea, are the beginning of the chain of life, the source of all food for every animal that lives there from single-celled ones to whales.

At the present time, the most pressing problem on earth is to feed the multiplying population, and to meet this ever-present challenge, we must study the sea. The oceans make world highways, are a storehouse of minerals and chemicals and even medicines, and give space for healthy recreation and release from crowded land.

The oceans can help us in our military defense if our knowledge of them is sufficient; or they can be the place in which our enemies' lurking nuclear submarines hide to attack us, if we remain in ignorance.

Oceanography is a broad science that encompasses many other disciplines of learning. It requires the application of physical and mathematical sciences to enable us to understand the interrelationships of air, water and solid land which together form the earth upon which we live.

A diver wearing self-contained underwater breathing apparatus (Scuba) has freedom to explore a group of different kinds of coral.

QUESTIONS ABOUT OUR EARTH

Once upon a time, four and one-half billion years ago, the newborn earth was hot, round and pockmarked by the turmoil within and without. There were no well-defined continental rises and no marked depressions in its surface. There was no water, no atmosphere as we know it, and, of course, no life. How did the distribution of continental elevations and oceanic depressions come about? How did the water fill the ocean basins? Were they filled slowly? Or was the mantle of water always about what it is today? How did the atmosphere's present composition come about? And how did life begin in the oceans? How did the chain of evolution begin and develop into the wealth of plant and animal life that we know on our planet today?

These are the primary questions of the natural history of our earth in which the oceans play a leading role. Eons ago, they were the birthplace of life itself. Even today, the oceans supply the moisture in our atmosphere, provide us with life-giving rain and temper our climate. Oceans are an unknown potential. They are an almost untapped source of food and minerals needed by man. As population on earth increases, the resources of the continents that poke out from beneath the water become strained to meet humanity's needs and, to support our life that began in the sea, we must once again turn to the sea.

Science, contrary to belief, gives no final answers. For each question answered by scientists, half a dozen others are raised. Thus, the many questions about the origins of our planet and universe multiply more quickly even than people! This is a fortunate thing; otherwise, the material on which to feed man's curiosity would dwindle. And so man with his theories supposes solutions, but nature continually proposes new problems.

In the Beginning

When the earth first began to form not long after the origin of the universe, it was not as compact as it is today; but gradually it shrank to its present size and degree of solidity. In fact, the diffuse protoplanet from which it formed may have had a hundred times the mass of material — consisting mostly of light gases — which, because of their violent motion, escaped to space. Only after this did our geologic record begin, and we date the age of the earth from that time. The age of the universe is estimated by observing the rate at which stars far, far away recede from each other. In receding, their light shifts to the longer wave length, red, just as the whistle of a departing train lowers in pitch as it speeds away. From this rate of spreading of the stars, we can calculate how long ago they were all close together.

How the Continents and Ocean Basins Grew

The Martian observer, from his distance, would not detect details of our coast lines. He would probably be struck by the curious symmetry of the planet, where water appears as the mirror image of land. He would discern four continents—the dominant pattern of three petal-like land areas stretching down from the Northern Hemisphere—the Americas, Europe-Africa and Asia-Australasia—the tips pointing toward, but not reaching, the fourth continent, Antarctica. Diametrically opposite, across the globe from each of the continents, he would see a corresponding ocean—the Arctic Ocean opposite the Antarctic continent, the Pacific Ocean opposite Europe-Africa, the Indian Ocean opposite the Americas and the Atlantic Ocean opposite Asia-Australasia. These oceans, too, he would see as petal-shaped, starting in the Southern Hemisphere and reaching upward toward the Arctic Ocean.

VIEW OF NORTHERN HEMISPHERE

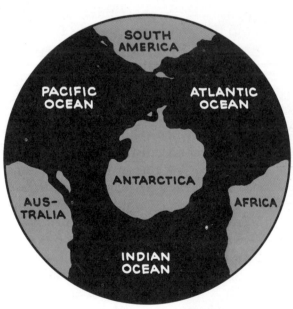

VIEW OF SOUTHERN HEMISPHERE

An observer from far out in space would be struck by the symmetry of our planet, where water appears as a mirror image of land. He would see in the Northern Hemisphere these petal-like land areas stretching southward around the equator. He would also see three great oceans stretching petal-like northward between the land masses.

An observer from space would see that the oceans dominate the Southern Hemisphere with three great petal-like extensions northward. Three land-masses separate the oceans.

Drawn especially for use in this book by Creative Educational Society, Inc.

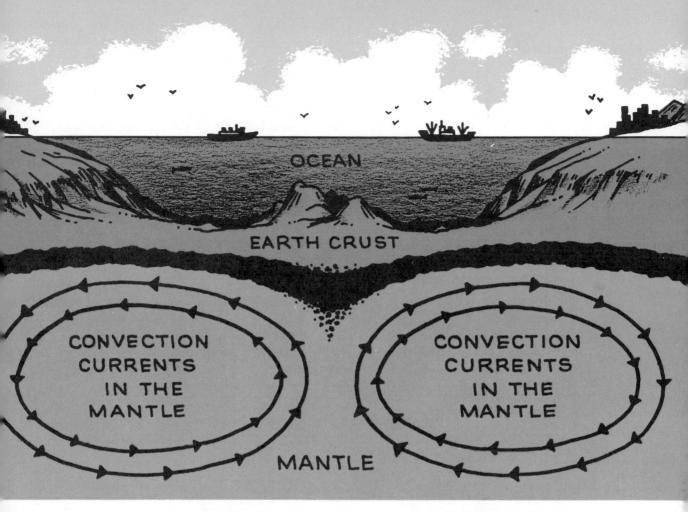

This drawing illustrates one theory of the formation of continents.

How the earth's crust developed continents and ocean basins is explained by some as due to the slow convection (that is, rising of hot material and sinking of colder) in cells of the semi-plastic material beneath. The continents were formed where three cells touched, and the flow toward each of their edges converged. The oceans similarly formed at the center where the flow outward toward the edges diverges, leaving a hollow. The cells meet at four of the corners of a cube making four continents. The cells diverge at the four other corners making four oceans. Notice that three of the continents are mostly in the Northern Hemi-sphere and the Antarctic continent at the South Pole with an ocean opposite each continent.

This would mean that during geologic time the continents have grown and the ocean basins have deepened. We find by measuring the decay of radio-active substances into stable ones (the same method that gives us the estimate of the four-and-one-half-billion-year age of the earth) that the oldest rocks are generally found toward the center of the continents, thus supporting the idea of slow growth around the edges, while the ocean basins contain "younger" or newer material brought up from the earth's interior.

How the Oceans Were Filled

One of the unsolved questions is whether the ocean waters and the atmosphere were formed before the beginning of geologic records or whether they grew slowly throughout time—squeezed out from our planet. In favor of the slow growth of the oceans theory is the fact that the rate of flow of water from volcanic springs at the present time is more than sufficient to have filled the oceans through geologic time. In a large area of the Pacific Ocean there are coral atolls and seamounts with their flat tops far below present sea level. These could have come about by a deepening of the ocean bottom from which they rise, or they could have resulted from an increase in the amount of water in the ocean basins, but most probably they are due to both of these causes. Some of this deepening seems to have taken place in the last hundred million years and so would indicate that perhaps a fourth of all ocean water has been squeezed to the surface of the earth by the turmoil within it in the last fortieth of its age. If the internal activity which causes this increase of water continues, we may have a completely water-covered planet after the next hundred million years.

A diagram showing a cross section of a coral atoll.

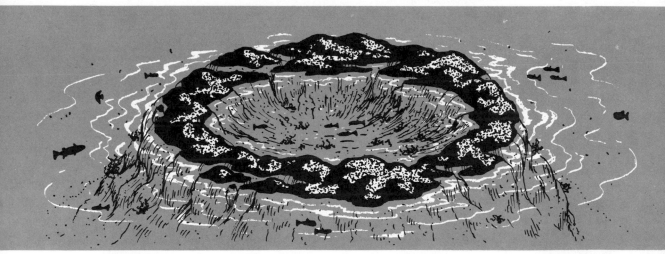

TOP VIEW ▲

▼ SIDE VIEW

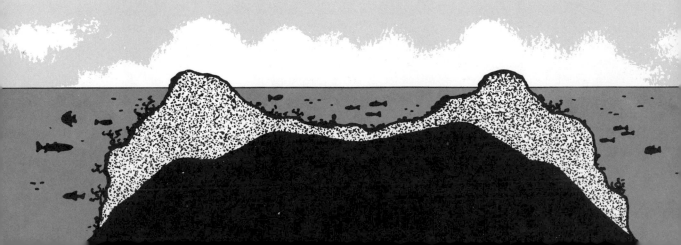

THE BOUNDARIES OF THE SEA

Let us look at a map of the oceans designed from an oceanographer's point of view. Ordinarily in your atlas you will find that, in order to skin an earth-like globe and flatten it out on a piece of paper, the cut that is needed is made within the oceans so that the land area is left undisturbed. You have, no doubt, seen maps of the world in an ellipse where the cut that forms the edge of the map is made along the middle of the Pacific Ocean. In the oceanographer's map the cut is made entirely within land so that the edge of the map is all land, and the oceans are seen as a single body of water.

In Genesis 1, Verse 9, "God said, 'Let the waters under the heaven be gathered together into one place' . . . and it was so." And so it is shown here; a single body of water with three great limbs, the Pacific, Atlantic and Indian Oceans, joined together by the circumpolar sea. The cut starts in Malaya, goes through Siberia, North America and terminates in Central America. It goes through the Bering Strait, but the Bering Strait is so shallow (about fifty feet) and so narrow that, from the oceanographer's point of view, it is insignificant and might just as well be dry land. Because there is no significant connection between the Arctic and Pacific Oceans, there are no icebergs in the North Pacific. The substantial connection of the Arctic Ocean is, as the map indicates, to the North Atlantic, which explains the large number of icebergs there.

Such a map, although it distorts, preserves equal areas so you can compare land areas with sea and appreciate the immense extent of the ocean. Two-thirds of the whole surface of the earth is covered with water — an area of 140 million square miles with an average depth of two and one-half miles.

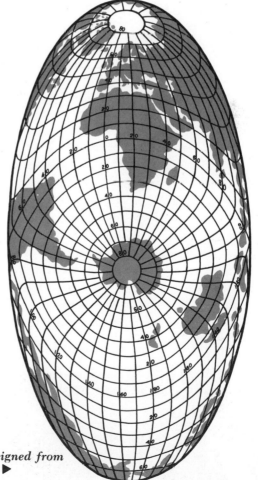

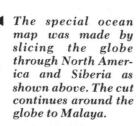

◄ The special ocean map was made by slicing the globe through North America and Siberia as shown above. The cut continues around the globe to Malaya.

This map of the world was designed from an oceanographic point of view. ►

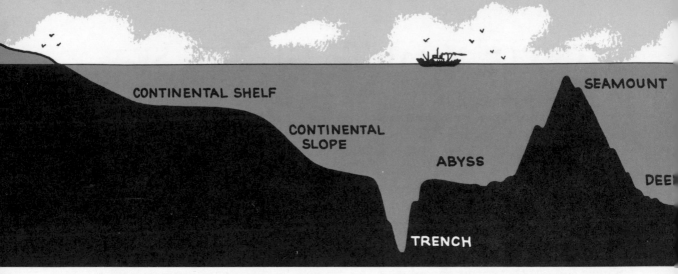

CONTINENTAL SHELF

CONTINENTAL SLOPE

SEAMOUNT

ABYSS

DEE

TRENCH

The sea floor is not level, but has features which on land would be called mountains, valleys, cliffs, and plateaus. This diagram of a cross-section of sea floor near the shore shows these features and their oceanographic names.

The sea bottom has four levels. Slanting from the land are the *continental shelves.* Then come steeper drops, the *continental slopes.* Very deep parts, half the ocean, are the *abyssal regions.* Deepest of all are great cracks in the sea floor called *trenches.* The deepest trench, the Mariana Trench off Guam, has a depth of about seven miles. That is deeper than Mount Everest is high and much deeper than any canyon on land.

In the continual cycle of water from the oceans to the continents, through the atmosphere and back to the sea via the rivers, land is continually being washed down into the sea. "All the rivers run into the sea; yet the sea is not full." If mountain-building forces under the seas were not counteracting these erosion processes to keep land's head above water, all the land would ultimately be washed into the sea. In that case, the whole earth would be completely covered by ocean waters to a depth of a mile and one-half. This gives some idea of the immense body of water from which data has to be gathered in order to present an adequate picture of the state of the oceans.

This vastness of the oceans contributes one of the ingredients that makes their study fascinating and causes the study of the oceans to be a combination of the ideas conjured in such word combinations as: science and art, invention and imagination, research and exploration, inquiry and probing into unknown reaches where man cannot go. These are the same ingredients which have made the literary epics of the sea. The science of the sea is an account of man's heroic struggle to understand better, and thus be able to withstand the majestic forces of the sea.

In this way, the science of the oceans discredits those who maintain that technological progress strips life of part of its charm. Quite the reverse — it opens up a world so fantastic that pure imagination could never conceive it. And in opening up the unknown recesses of our planet, it becomes a "great adventure" which gives raw materials for literature, poetry and further research.

Part Two

OCEANOGRAPHY

EARLY HISTORY OF OCEANOGRAPHY

Oceanography, like any other science, begins with observation and, to observe the sea, we must go upon it and into it. "To go to sea" is a phrase that still has a ring of adventure at any age, in any country. So, the first oceanographer was the brave man who sat astride a log and set out on the water. Perhaps the log tipped over, so later someone bound two logs together to make a raft or, even better, separated the logs with outriggers to keep them from overturning. Still later, logs were hollowed so that a man's weight was below the point of buoyancy and the boat was as stable as a pendulum.

These rafts and boats drifted with the wind. Then crude sails helped the drift but were not able to make headway against the wind. The early ships that went between North Africa and India used nature's natural see-saw of the winds — the monsoon — to take them back and forth. Paddles and oars used to go against the wind have been found dating back to 7,000 B.C., but the rudder, enabling the boat to change direction with a sail, came much later.

Courageous seafarers in ancient vessels made maps of the edges of the ocean as far as they dared sail. The shape of the Mediterranean Sea, surrounded by land (hence its name), was very well shown on the earliest maps. But beyond the surrounding land early sailors believed there was a terrifying, endless sea. In other parts of the world, explorers had glimpses of the shape of their nearby seas. As in a theater when the curtain opens a few feet, people in different locations saw different parts of the scene. Only much later was the geographical curtain fully drawn back, revealing the boundaries of the ocean as a whole.

The early voyages of exploration were remarkable because, though latitude was estimated from the length of the shadow a stick cast when the sun was at its zenith, there was no way of measuring longitude. Good maps were made just from the direction and estimated distance sailed. The most important invention for navigation (and oceanography) was the escapement clock and its offspring, the first marine chronometer, because without knowing the time, longitude could not be measured; but with a timekeeper and the natural heavenly bodies, it could be. Even today, oceanographic research in areas such as the circumpolar Antarctic Sea is hindered when clouds hide the stars and sun.

Modern navigational systems tell a vessel's position from the difference of time at which two radio signals, sent out simultaneously from two separated land transmitters, are received at the ship. Man-made satellites are also used for navigation so that we can know where we are even in long periods of overcast skies. It is interesting that even these modern navigational devices are limited by a timing problem — the uncertainty of scientists to know for sure the time it takes for a radio

For thousands of years man has taken food from the sea.

pulse to go to and fro as it is bent along unknown paths by ionization in the air.

At the time of the two-dimensional exploration of the seas, oceanographic and geographic explorations were one. To define the boundaries of the land also defined the boundaries of the sea.

Ferdinand Magellan, a Portuguese sea captain organized the first expedition to circumnavigate the globe. He left Spain in 1519 with 5 ships and 236 men and proved that by always sailing westward you could travel completely around the world.

In 1763, nearly 245 years after Magellan's voyage, a British naval officer and explorer, Captain James Cook, while conducting a charting survey of the Southern Hemisphere, showed that Australia (so named because it was believed to be the southernmost continent) was, on the contrary, separate from any continent that might lie at the South Pole. Captain Cook's voyage made great contributions to geography and botany, but as he sought to withstand the sea and use the winds to traverse it from island to island, he ignored the sea itself and the life in it.

Man's knowledge of life in the sea in early days was confined to the fish taken for food near the surface and on the edges of the sea. Such deep-sea creatures as the giant squid were so rarely seen that in the minds of people who saw them they conjured up frightening tales of sea monsters which could devour a whole ship.

The Phoenicians and the people of the Malay Peninsula used a kind of "sonar" in those early days. A man would put his head or an ear trumpet under water to listen for the honking of fish, and then would herd the fish together by beating underwater drums. The fishing methods and nets used today are similar to those used over two thousand years ago. But life in the depths of the sea has only been studied in the last century or so. Until then it was thought to exist only in the upper layers of the ocean.

In 1842, Edward Forbes brought up some sea life from 800 feet. Then, about 1850, the Norwegian vessel *Michael Sars* found the first deep-sea monsters. They were very strange in appearance to the people who had seen only the fish from the surface layers. Interestingly enough, when pictures of these odd forms of life were widely published in magazines, the Lochness monster was claimed to have been sighted in Scotland.

To jump to the present day — and you may draw whatever parallel you wish — it is only now, after our technology is on the brink of interplanetary travel, that we interpret phenomena in the sky as flying saucers. Apparently each age, with the colossal egocentricity of man, interprets what it sees in the light of its most recent findings.

The **Oceanographer** *a modern oceanographic research ship. Operated by the U. S. Coast and Geodetic Survey. Commissioned in 1966, this ship has many features specifically designed to facilitate research activity.*

The research vessel **Te Vega** *off the coast of New Guinea, 1963.*

21

To return to the early history of oceanography, in 1860 a broken telegraph cable in the Mediterranean was brought up and was found to have shellfish clinging to it from a depth of over one thousand fathoms. Such clues led Charles Wyville Thompson to work at greater depths, first in the *Lightening* and then in the *Porcupine,* from which he netted large quantities of marine life from depths of fifteen thousand feet. The results inspired him to organize the *Challenger* expedition which was the first extended deep-sea exploratory voyage of the world's oceans. The expedition left Portsmouth, England in 1872, and during the next four years, sailed nearly 69,000 nautical miles on every ocean except the Arctic Ocean and stopped at every continent except Antarctica.

With its nets, trawls and bottom-scrapers, discovered and identified more than 4,700 new species of sea life, more than any expedition since has been able to discover. During the voyage, soundings were made down to 27,000 feet which led to the discovery of the 36,000 feet deep Mariana Trench near Guam in the Pacific Ocean (named the Challenger Deep) now considered the deepest place in the world. After the Challenger expedition returned to England in 1876, it took scientists nearly twenty-three years to compile and publish all of the data collected into fifty books containing nearly 30,000 pages.

This pioneering voyage firmly established Oceanography as a vital and necessary science.

This world map shows the four year voyage taken by the **Challenger** *expedition.*

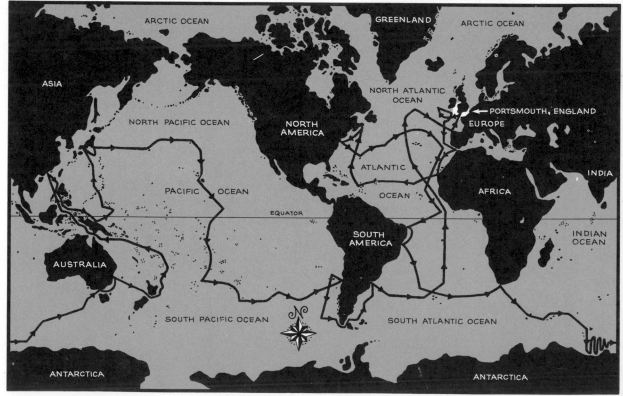

The most famous of all research vessels was the H.M.S. Challenger which from 1872 to 1876 carried an expedition around the world led by C. W. Thompson. The H.M.S. Challenger was a three-masted, spar-deck corvette of 2306 ton displacement and auxiliary engines of 1234 horsepower.

23

LATER VESSELS AND OBSERVATIONS

The *Challenger* set a pattern for exploring the depths of the sea. Her observations gave world-wide charts of surface and deep-sea temperatures. Chemical analyses of thousands of water samples showed that the proportion of the various salts in the sea is relatively constant even though the total saltiness varies. This formed the basis for telling total salinity from analysis of the chlorides alone.

The success of the *Challenger* expedition led to many others. In the United States Navy, the *Albatross* was built and later the *Carnegie*, a vessel of wood and nonmagnetic materials for surveying the earth's magnetism. Other ships were built for special purposes. Fridtjof Nansen designed the *Fram* with a hull that, when pinched in the Arctic ice, would rise up instead of being crushed. Though his attempt to drift his ship frozen in the ice to the North Pole did not succeed, the scientific work and instrumental methods set another nautical milestone.

If this brief history of attempts to explore the seas has interested you, you may appreciate the following recipe for an oceanographer: "Add to the curiosity and doubt which breeds the research scientist, the adventurousness of the explorer, and keep well stirred." Such a man must be intensely curious about the part of the earth he is studying and he must enjoy overcoming the rigorous conditions under which he may need to work in order to gather his data.

Research Vessel, Atlantis II, at Woods Hole Oceanographic Institution.

Research vessel Vema *of Columbia University Lamont Geophysical Observatory.*

Working on the Vema on a rough day.

WE MUST SEE THE OCEAN TO UNDERSTAND IT

With our instruments and vehicles, we must be able to see through the ocean to understand it. Best of all is to go down into it and use our senses directly! Scientific instruments extend the range of our senses, and vehicles extend the reach of our arms and legs. By instruments alone we know something of the distant space about us where we have never been. Similarly, we know a little about the deep ocean by the probings of instruments on long wires. Instruments can detect the whole of the electro-magnetic spectrum from the longest radio waves to the shortest gamma and X-rays, including the narrow range encompassed by our eyes. These instruments can hear above or below the pitch to which our ears are tuned, measure pressures too small to feel or too great for us to withstand, and analyze substances far more accurately than we can do by natural taste and smell. The eyes are of little use where there is little to see, as in space. Therefore, man in space is only a repairman of the sensing instruments transmitting information to earth, or an experimental animal, or a spacecraft chauffeur until he can land on an extraterrestrial body. But ultimately all recorded bits of information are put into the scientist's brain through his eyes. In unexplored regions where there is so much to see, there is great advantage in having a watcher on the spot who can observe, draw upon his memory and develop an exploration plan as the scene unfolds. The ocean is such a region.

A plankton net alongside the research vessel Eltanin. Some plankton nets are made of mesh even finer than that pictured and can catch very tiny organisms.

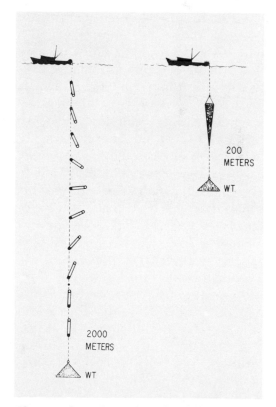

The vessel on the right is lowering a sampling net to a pre-determined depth. The vessel on the left has lowered a series of special devices, called Nansen Bottles, which are used to collect samples of water at specific depths.

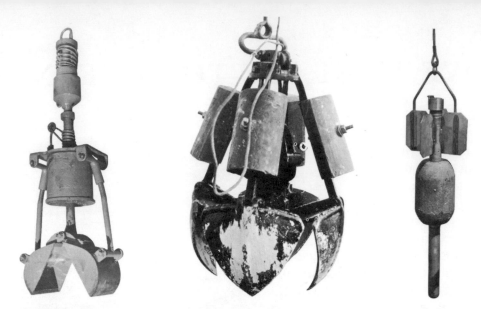

These three instruments are used for collecting study materials from the ocean floor. All three carry heavy weights which help to push them into the bottom material. The instruments at left and center have jaw-like devices which snap shut around the sample. The instrument at the right is hollow and when driven into the ocean floor collects a long cylindrical plug or "core." A good core sample will show the various layers of the sand, silt, or like materials, and other substances, as they are found on the ocean bottom.

Next to the ship, the most important piece of equipment is a winch—a drum with miles of wire that can be laid out and hauled in—to carry bottom samplers and corers to the ocean floor, to suspend thermometers, water samplers and other instruments at any depth, and to haul the biologists' nets. The vessel extends the oceanographer's stride at sea; the winch wire extends his reach downward so that the instruments can sense and bring up information from the depths. Temperature and salinity measurements make it possible for him to compute the density of the water, from which he can study currents, the origin of water types, and internal waves.

A most interesting and intriguing problem not appreciated by most people is the whole problem of sea level. The term "sea level" is misleading because the sea is very far from level. Even if it is completely waveless, and disregarding the rhythmic breathing of the sea that is exhibited in the tides—even if these regular irregularities can be eliminated—the sea is far from level. It has hills and valleys in it much as the land does (except the hills and valleys in the sea surface are very much smaller), and these hills and valleys relate to the system of the oceans' currents. Differences of a very few inches of height in the average sea surface are extremely important from the point of view of ocean currents and their variations. It is easy to see the connection between currents and the slope of the sea surface by remembering the well-known fact that water runs downhill. So it does in the sea. The surface water of the sea tries to flow from a region of high sea surface to a region of lower sea surface. Due to the turning of the earth and consequent interplay of the so-called Coriolis force, the actual motion, when it reaches a steady state, is such that the current runs parallel to the contours of the sea surface.

The great clock-wise whirl of water that we call the Gulf Stream, which flows in an elliptical kind of path around the Sargasso Sea, moves in such a fashion that sea level must be higher in the center of this whirl — at the Azores — than at any place on the edge, such as Miami. But one of the unsolved problems of geodesy (the science which deals with measurements of the figure of the earth) is that we have as yet no way of relating mean sea level on one continent to mean sea level on another or on islands separated widely by water.

Below the level of no motion there are far, far slower currents, and these currents are even more difficult to measure. The slowest of all is the drift of the bottom water, which flows into all the open oceans from the Antarctic circumpolar sea. The water that is left after the ice freezes near the Antarctic ice cap in the fall is the heaviest water in the oceans. As ice freezes, it excludes salt — it freezes at slightly above the ordinary freezing point of pure water — so that the water that is left when sea-ice forms is the most saline water there is, and also the coldest. It is therefore the densest, sinking to the bottom and seeping northwards, and is found at the bottommost level, even in the northern parts of all three oceans.

New tools involving the use of radioactive tracers may make it much simpler for us to follow the current systems, especially the slow ones, and one may speculate that a knowledge of these very slow currents with their different temperatures will aid in the ultimate long-term prediction of weather trends.

Ocean currents of the world.

One of the very important things to the physical oceanographer is to know the density of sea water. This density is a combination of the temperature and the saltiness of the sea. To measure the temperature at depths away from the surface requires a thermometer with a memory, and reversing thermometers were developed for this purpose. They were sent down to the depth required, allowed to acquire the temperature there, and then turned upside down by a messenger which slid down the wire. This procedure was time-consuming and caused the vessel to be stationary for long periods of time.

For the surface layers of the sea, where changes are rapid, various instruments have been developed in the last twenty years which can be used while the ship is moving. The bathythermograph, which falls freely at the end of a thin piano wire, records temperature against depth when trailed from any vessel traveling at full speed. The same instrument used with water bottles, which can be automatically closed at preset depths, can collect water samples at the same time. Water samples are analyzed for nutrient salts, dissolved gases, and other properties of sea water pertinent to the particular research. Nets can vary from meshes fine enough to filter tiny plankton to coarser deep-sea trawls or nets that scrape the bottom. These are all used to collect samples of sea life.

Continuous samplers which deposit the plankton on a continually moving sheet of muslin give systematic collections for the biologist. Even currents can now be measured from a moving ship by towing electrodes behind a vessel along a zigzagging course. These and other similar measurements help us to observe rapid changes — the ocean's weather rather than its climate. The synoptic or simultaneous bird's-eye view of an ocean area that they provide is most important to ocean forecasting. Now extensions of these rapid measuring methods feed data into electronic recording and computing devices located on board ship and at central oceanographic data processing centers on land.

Invented by the author in 1937, the bathythermograph has been an important tool in oceanographic research. Lowered from a moving ship, this instrument provides a continuous record of depth and temperature data.

Ice is a great obstacle for surface ships. Here three ships of the U. S. Navy move an iceberg blocking the supply channel to McMurdo Station, Antarctica.

The ice-covered oceans are explored through icebreakers which laboriously clear passages by riding on the ice, breaking it by sheer weight, and then fanning it out behind with their great propellers. Oceanographic observations have been made in the water below the ice from floating ice islands in the Arctic, but only wherever they happen to drift. Now atomic submarines go under the ice, using sonar and television devices which not only guard against obstructions but can also look downward, sideways and upward to find cracks and leads through which the submarine can surface. A combination of the submarine and modern instruments now makes it possible to study the water under the ice. Buoys which float at predetermined depth can be followed by a submarine using sonar so that the currents in the Arctic Sea can be measured.

Submarines are able to cruise beneath the ice and surface where there is an opening. Here the U.S.S. Perch encounters a peculiar ice formation called "pancake ice" in the Bering Sea off the Coast of Alaska.

The Bottom of the Sea

To measure the depth of the sea a lead formerly was used on the end of a hemp rope. The word "fathom" comes from the root "to embrace"— from the picture of a seaman's outstretched arms as he measured each six-foot span. The first deep sounding with this method was made by Sir James Ross in 1840. Later, greater depths were plumbed with a weight on the end of a thin piano wire unreeled and reeled by a power-driven winch. But even this was tedious, and soundings were scattered so that early bathymetric charts did not show the cliffs, seamounts, ridges, canyons, and plains as we know them today. About 1923, echo sounding revolutionized depth measurement; a noise maker was placed in the vessel's hull to emit a "ping" and the time it took for the echo to return from the bottom was noted. Instead of one thousand soundings a year, five thousand could be made in a day. All kinds of ships on the high seas now keep echo sounders running constantly and record the bottom topography automatically. These measurements give us the maps of the sea floor, which are used by mariners and submariners, just as an airplane pilot on a clear day knows his position from the land features he can see below. Underwater movie and television cameras let us see what is going on in the depths. With their own light sources and with underwater sound to position them and click the shutter, these cameras can operate in the greatest depths.

An underwater camera is lowered over the side of the research vessel Eltanin. Cameras like this must provide their own lights. Operation may be either automatic or remote.

To observe below the ocean bottom, coring tubes are used. They sometimes pierce through a hundred feet of sediment and bring up the layered cores which tell the earth's history. Newer drilling devices promise to extend the information about ocean-bottom cores by thousands of feet. At these depths, scientists can learn about the interior of the earth by placing explosive charges and seismographs on the sea floor and studying the patterns of the earth waves as they are slowed, accelerated, and bent by the different layers. The flow of heat from the interior of the earth outward can be measured miles down at the bottom of the sea more easily than on land

Here on board the Eltanin *several hundred core samples await analysis. Each sample is sealed in the tube in which it was collected.*

because the deep sea is a natural thermostat. A probe in the sediments, which measures the temperature at two different depths, and a core from which the heat conductivity can be measured, provide the data to calculate the amount of heat flowing out. From such data geophysicists speculate on the origin of continents and oceans — some evidence indicating that parts of the sea floor are "young" material, extruded comparatively recently from deeper down in the earth's interior, or mantle.

In 1961, a drilling barge let down a drill through twelve thousand feet of water near Guadalupe in the Pacific and penetrated more than five hundred feet of sediment into the hard underlying basalt. Drilling with the two-mile length of rod, which was only inches in diameter, was like drilling by twisting a long, flexible thread. The barge was kept close to the area above the hole by driving the appropriate propellers of four outboard motors. These held the barge to a fixed position with reference to anchored marker buoys kept in sight by radar. So successful was this first experiment that drilling far into the bottom is now being done or is planned in many places in the oceans.

THE OCEAN AS FRIEND OR FOE

The oceans have been represented as fearsome things. The earliest maps always showed the known land girdled by a ring of impenetrable seas. Just as forests were the cover for ambush in mortal conflicts of an earlier age, so the oceans of today are the recesses where modern fighting submarines can hide and surprise. Indians could win battles against superior weapons because by their woodlore they could read signs and track enemies while they themselves moved silently and left no trace. The forest was transparent to them, but it hid them from the eyes of their enemies. So it is today in submarine warfare. We try to develop instruments that make the oceans transparent to us so that we can "see" our enemies; yet we want to develop our own submarines and instruments to a point where they are undetectable by others.

Conditions on the surface of the ocean, weather and currents have been important in strategy and tactics in naval warfare from the earliest times. The first naval interest in oceanography came in the days of sailing ships. Sailing directions go back at least two thousand years, but it was not until the 1850's that Lieutenant Maury compiled the experiences written in navigators' logs on the winds, the currents, and the tides to start the first sailing charts.

Until World War II, naval interest was two-dimensional. Although underwater sound was used for detecting ships and submarines in World War I, real interest in that third dimension developed much later. In the late 1930's, it was recognized that changes of temperature with depth bent the sound rays, and that these changes had both time and space variations at sea which had to be measured and, if possible, predicted if ranges of sound transmission were to be foretold.

The bathythermograph, operating from a moving ship, could draw a chart showing how the temperature changes with depth. This contribution to "seeing and remaining unseen" showed naval submariners in which layers the noises of their own engines were transmitted least. It showed them how they could adjust their buoyancy — make the submarine's density greater than the water above it and less than that below it, so it could balance in silence between different layers of the sea. It provided them with an idea of the best depths for attack and the best depths for evasion.

Since early times man's love and fear of the sea have forced him to build sturdy vessels to conquer it. Now while a destroyer plows through heavy seas in the Atlantic, an atomic submarine may glide smoothly and silently on its mission, unaffected by surface conditions.

The theory of water waves has been known for many years—how the distance between crests shortens as they roll up in shallower water—and what depths of water cause them to break into white-caps coming in to the shore. The navigators of amphibious landing craft can chart, from aerial photographs, unknown underwater contours of enemy beaches. Even the apparent random interplay of waves in the open sea is studied to provide some kind of prediction in connection with stabilizing and aiming missiles either from surface or submarine vessels.

The submarine navigator must know the shape of the ocean bottom in order to see the enemy without being seen and to be able to find his way. This means that he must have maps showing the contours of hills and valleys, ridges and trenches, and the nature of the bottom—whether it is a good mirror for sound waves or a poor one. The mid-Atlantic ridge beneath the sea, probably the greatest mountain range on earth, may look entirely different from continental mountains because it has never been subjected to such severe processes of erosion. As Maury charted surface currents and winds, today oceanographers chart the speed and direction of currents at all depths in the oceans. Great subsurface rivers, equivalent to a thousand Mississippis, have been found underneath such huge surface currents as the Gulf Stream and its counterparts in other oceans. As we get differences of gravity on land due to the presence of mountains, valleys and plains and the different material in them, so gravity varies in the ocean. Charts of its variation and that of the earth's magnetic field are a further aid to navigators.

Airplanes flying over land now seldom use the earlier navigational methods. In ordinary flying, the country is criss-crossed by radio beams—tracks along which the airplane runs unerringly to its destination. On land, we have networks of radar which plot the positions of all aircraft to prevent collisions and to detect intruders. The counterpart of these criss-crossed networks for the sea are submarine beacons radiating sound beams for the guidance of underwater craft as the lighthouse uses a light beam to guide ships on the surface. Sound receivers must be coupled together in a vast underwater spider web of millions of miles of cables, which, like our radar surveillance in the air space, can keep track continuously of normal comings and goings, and yet single out any stranger in our midst. To identify friend from foe is one of the most difficult underwater problems the Navy has.

WIND →

The pattern waves make as they break on the beach is affected by the contours of the ocean floor near the shore. An expert can describe the channels, bars, and other features of an unfamiliar shore by studying its waves.

Radar installations in the sea extend our range of surveillance in the air around our continent, but cannot penetrate the ocean water. However, artificial islands like this, built on continental shelves or in other shallows provide bases for many types of oceanographic research activities.

STATIONS IN THE SEA

In studying our planet we have to know the geographical distribution of its physical and biological make-up. But we also need to know how time changes many things at one and the same place. On land we watch the response of animals and trees to the changing of seasons in one locality. From any one place we can relate animal behavior and plant response to the varying conditions of the weather recorded by instruments over a period of time. But in the oceans, comparatively few series of measurements from ships anchored for more than a few days have been made until recently. Measurements of the time variations of temperature, salinity, currents, light, correlated with biological observations of the variations of plankton and fish populations at a fixed position over a long period, are extremely revealing.

Stimulated by the search for oil under the continental shelves and by the need of a warning network against intruding enemy aircraft, engineers built artificial islands on the continental shelves in the sea. These were the first stations in the sea, and artificial islands of this kind may be built on many of the shoals in the oceans or rise from the top of seamounts that reach up nearly to the surface. In very deep water the next step is to anchor ordinary surface ships for long periods and study the changes with time.

This tower, built for the Naval Electronics Laboratory collects a variety of oceanographic information.

Oil rigs mounted on barges are used for drilling exploratory wells in shallow offshore areas. New floating platforms have now been built which permit drilling in six hundred feet of water.

For many purposes, an oceanographic vessel must anchor and make a station at sea. Anchoring in deep water was at one time difficult, not because the motion of the ship broke the wire, but because the very weight of miles of wire broke itself. The German vessel *Meteor,* in the 1930's, anchored in about four miles of water using a wire tapered toward the bottom to reduce this strain. Today, plastic rope with the same weight as sea water, and therefore without weight in water, makes anchoring easier. Furthermore, instead of anchoring the ship, marker buoys can be anchored and the ship's position maintained very accurately under power with reference to them.

In some coastal areas, permanent platforms, or drilling islands, are built. Most of these operate in less than two hundred feet of water.

This strange craft is actually an instrument buoy in towing position named Flip (Floating Instrument Platform). It is large enough to carry a crew.

Next to come were the vertical floating tubes hundreds of feet long, standing on end, heavy on the bottom and projecting a few feet into the air at the top. These can be moored in one place. The men live in these tall buoys floating in the sea and watch and record the physical and biological interplay. In the not-too-distant future permanent stations of this kind will be scattered all over the oceans. Not only will they be useful for understanding the sea, but they will be mid-ocean lighthouses and emergency shelters for submarine or surface ocean travelers and fishermen.

The same buoy in its upright position is shown in use in the ocean off San Diego.

As well as these anchored buoys, there will be manned, drifting buoys traveling slowly with the currents and numerous unmanned ones at surface, mid-depth and bottom. These will automatically radio their measurements via satellite to central storage-computing and analysis centers, either on land or at sea.

These networks of buoys in and on the sea will need to be supplied, attended, and have their data collected. Aircraft flying above the sea also will be used to gather information about the oceans. From an aircraft at high speed, a view of the ocean can show currents, wind streaks, boundaries between water of different kinds, and concentrations of marine life. Also, the buoys in the sea can transmit their data from the depths, first by sound to the surface and then by radio to an aircraft flying above them. The airplane will be able to question many buoys at the same time and get a simultaneous bird's-eye picture of the situation.

Buoys fitted with appropriate instruments can provide data concerning temperature, salinity, depth, currents, and other important features of the sea. This one is maintained by the Woods Hole Oceanographic Institution, Woods Hole, Massachusetts.

PHYKOS

CT 7705 H

Airplanes, too, can drop measuring instruments which, as they sink down into the depths, will transmit the conditions of the different layers through which they pass. We may expect to see large mother ships letting down bathyscaphes and sending up helicopters to gather the total data that we will need about the sea. Not only these special vehicles for oceanographic research, but also ocean liners and fishing vessels can be equipped with continuous recording instruments which, without interfering with their normal business, can chart temperatures, salinities, abundance of plant and animal plankton, and fish populations. Only by the use of all of these can we hope to obtain a world map of the huge

Small deep-diving craft like the Asherah *have a cruising range of only twenty or thirty miles, but can be transported by a mother ship to wherever their special talents are required.*

oceans relating their physical conditions to the distribution of life in them. This map will give us the basis to understand complicated relationships and enable us to make useful predictions for fisheries, ocean travel, and for underwater communications. Out of it will come many other uses of ocean forecasting. All these together will provide the network of observations of both ocean and atmospheric conditions necessary for the weather predictions that we have today and for the electronic oceanic forecasting computers.

This map shows lines of equal distance from land at spacings of 300 nautical miles.

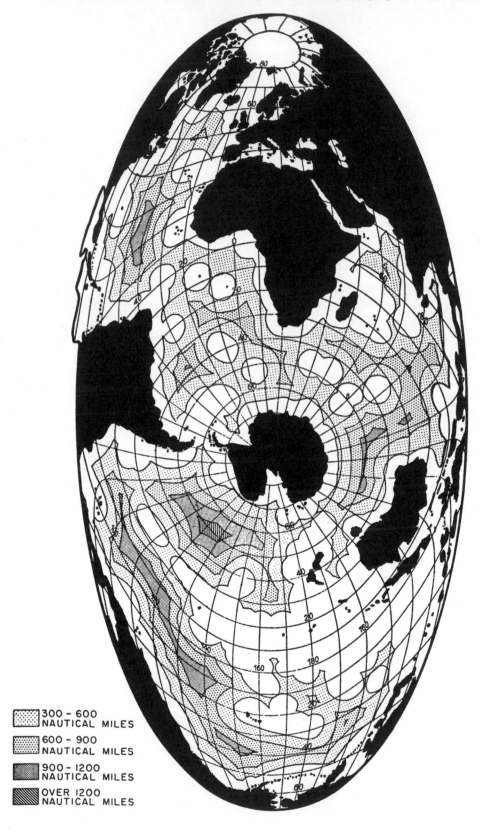

300 – 600
NAUTICAL MILES

600 – 900
NAUTICAL MILES

900 – 1200
NAUTICAL MILES

OVER 1200
NAUTICAL MILES

PLATFORMS IN THE SEA

We need to develop and use new kinds of observational platforms. "Platforms" is a well chosen word because it dissociates our thinking from the traditional idea of ships and can refer to ships, buoys, artificial islands and all the different configurations which can be used for the different things that we are going to do upon and under the sea.

In the 1940's, the author pointed out there was a requirement "for a specially designed floating vessel, manned or unmanned, which can be suitably anchored even in great depths of water" to fill the needs of the ocean world weather network. Later, there was a bill in the Senate to authorize the Coast Guard to construct an experimental nonpropelled seagoing ocean station. The bill was subsequently withdrawn. The world network is still completely inadequate for the electronics computers.

In the meantime, many other uses for these floating platforms have developed as ocean forecasting comes of age.

Now we know new designs and configurations for buoys, how to stabilize them, how to anchor them, how to protect them against fouling, how to telemeter the data, and how to power them for long periods by radioisotope atomic power, wave energy, or otherwise.

Our buoys can take meteorological, as well as oceanographic observations, and they can take measurements down into the deep water by sensors which travel up and down below the buoys. There are important uses for free-floating buoys, but we must learn how to track and

to locate them to know where they are and remove the hazard they present to navigation. We should find ways to turn them into assets by making them the beacons, seamarks and emergency stations to help the future vessels at sea.

Thus oceanography progresses from ships to buoys, to much more sophisticated platforms, and ultimately to floating factories, dwellings, and all the components of future ocean cities.

"Live" Maps

Traditionally, oceanographic data has been presented on maps or vertical cross-sections of the ocean in atlases. With the automatic data processing of huge amounts of oceanographic data, the future map may be entirely different. It may be a huge television-type screen on which you can call up from the data stored in the machine's memory a display of whatever data you happen to be interested in. Within seconds, tables containing writing and numbers or contour maps of the bottom of the sea will appear and you will be able to ask the computer to give you more detailed information on any particular point. Suppose you are looking at a full-color map of the North Atlantic temperature zones. You will be able to draw a line that projects a beam of light across the Gulf Stream and then instruct the machine to display the vertical section showing temperatures where you drew the line. The live atlas will be automatically self-revising as new data comes into the processing center.

OCEAN FORECASTING

Although we occasionally poke fun at the weatherman, there is no doubt that weather forecasts save lives and money in untold amounts each year. To forecast ocean weather conditions will be increasingly important as mankind turns more to the sea. Ocean and atmosphere work together, each influencing the other, so that improved oceanographic forecasts and better information of sea conditions can improve weather predictions; and better weather predictions, such as being able to foretell the strength of the winds over the sea, will improve the predictions of waves, surf, and swell. Benjamin Franklin recognized in his day that mail to England took one day less than the other way and he spoke of the "river in the sea," the Gulf Stream, of which we can *see* the edges and *feel* the cold on one side and warmth on the other. Accurate prediction of these factors reduces transoceanic crossing times, increases passenger comfort, reduces ship maintenance and repair costs,

and saves ships and the lives of men. Knowing the strength of a wind and how long a distance it takes to generate waves lets us predict the height and pounding of the waves a vessel may expect to encounter.

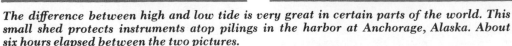

The difference between high and low tide is very great in certain parts of the world. This small shed protects instruments atop pilings in the harbor at Anchorage, Alaska. About six hours elapsed between the two pictures.

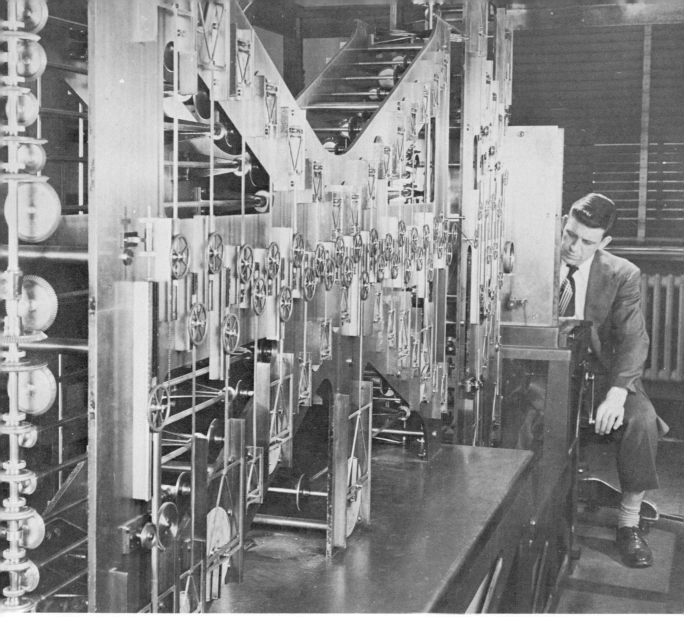

Today we are accustomed to electronic devices which can interpret all types of data. This tide predictor, however, is entirely mechanical and machines similar to it have been in use for many years.

Prediction of Tides

The rising and falling of the sea that we observe in the high and low tides is a phenomenon that can be forecast most accurately. This is because the tide-generating forces are governed by the precise and highly predictable motions of earth, sun, moon and other bodies in our planetary system. The tide periods can be broken down from a long record at any place into regular cyclic ones, reconstructed and projected into the future. Tides for coastal points can be predicted although local geography makes such predictions quite complicated. Prediction of tides can be extended to offshore effects which cause tidal currents, stir up nutrients, cause temperature changes, and thus affect sea life.

Icebergs can be a serious and deadly threat to any vessel on the sea. An international ice patrol service maintains constant watch in iceberg areas and provides bulletins concerning iceberg positions to all vessels.

Forecasting Ice and Icebergs

Another particular ocean forecast that has been used for many years is the prediction of the coming and going of ice in northern seas. Ice forecasting was highly developed quite a long time ago in the Baltic Sea. Because of the great amount of trade that went in and out of its numerous ports, it was important to know in advance when the ports would be open or closed by ice.

A more menacing kind of ice in the ocean, the treacherous floating icebergs, which show only a small fraction of their huge bulk above water, also has been watched and predicted for some time. Since the *Titanic* collided with an iceberg in a disaster that shocked the world, an international ice patrol service has studied conditions, made forecasts, and issued warnings to steer ships clear of this danger. To do this, the time and amount of calving of the icebergs from glaciers are studied; and the currents that carry them down in the Baffin Bay area are watched beyond the Grand Banks where they cross the main shipping lanes, right to their final melting as they meet the eddying fringes of the warm Gulf Stream.

Fish Forecasting

How the surface winds affect the production of food on which fish graze, and how these winds affect the infant mortality of the fish, establishes a basis for fish forecasting. One remarkable example of the value of forecasting can be found in haddock fishing on Georges banks off the coast of Cape Cod, Massachusetts. Here the strength and duration of offshore winds during the haddock's annual spawning period make it possible to predict three years in advance the probable size of the harvest of three-year-old fish. Wave and fish forecasts depend on knowing from the weatherman the winds over the sea. Forecasts will become more accurate as the observing network is improved. Wind divergencies predicted on a day-to-day basis can show fishermen where to go.

Vertical movements — upwellings due to wind divergence — and the stirring at the boundary between currents are two ways in which nature plows or overturns sea nutrients from lower layers to the top. At the surface of the sea the algae grass uses these nutrients. The best fishing grounds are where this upwelling and stirring take place.

Sound Forecasting

In the oceans we use sound waves for communication and for echo-sounding the depth of the ocean bottom. They are also used for the detection of intruding submarines and for locating schools of fish. Good or poor sound transmission depends on the distribution of temperature and salinity and the location of mys-

Information about ocean currents and weather conditions are indispensable to the fishing industry. Combined with knowledge of the biology of a fish species, this information can help locate fishing sites, and even predict fishing possibilities for future seasons. These tuna fishermen seem to have found productive waters.

terious scattering layers and other conditions that can be measured. The ionosphere, influenced by the sun, affects our ability to communicate by radio through atmosphere. Just as a central radio propagation laboratory predicts and recommends the best wave length, so can ocean forecasting predict physical conditions in the sea that affect sound.

Predicting Strength of Currents

Changes of major ocean currents, themselves partly driven by the winds, are much slower than those of the weather. Therefore, predictions about them assist long-range weather forecasting. Oceanographic forecasting has the advantage that these changes are slow, and even if unreliable at first, their usefulness and wide application will make the world ocean forecasting as common as weather forecasting.

Part III

MAN AND THE SEA

Its great flukes momentarily clearing the water, a whale heads for the deep. Whale species of commercial value have been practically exterminated from parts of their former range and are nowhere abundant.

LIFE IN THE SEA

To explain life in the sea, we must understand its origin, its evolution, and its total relationship in the cycle of sunshine and nutrients to plants, to grazing animals, to predators, and back to nutrients through the action of bacteria. We must understand also the linking of life in the sea to birds and land animals, including the greatest predator, man.

Life began in the oceans and has continued there far longer than it has existed in air or on land. Every living thing on earth finds its earliest forebears there. But because the ocean performs for life the same function it performs for our climate—namely, it acts as a steadying flywheel with no marked or rapid changes—the challenge for development of new species is not as great as on land. Naturally, rates of evolution in the ocean have not been as rapid. In spite of the much longer time life has existed in sea water and the fact that there is more ocean than land, only twenty per cent of all the species alive today are in the ocean. The rate of evolution is much faster on land because species must adapt to the more widely varying and rigorous conditions there. The drives of sex, hunger and thirst cause a variety from which nature selects the most adaptable. Evolution speeds up to produce, for example, a desert rat that can flourish on a diet so dry that other animals would die of thirst.

In places that are alternately wet and dry, such as shorelines where the oceans and land meet and the tides rhythmically submerge the beach

The sea provides livelihood for thousands of different kinds of crustaceans, including crabs, lobsters, and various shrimp like this "Krill." Much magnified in this photograph, these inch-long animals feed on even tinier organisms (plankton) and are in turn fed on by larger creatures, including the largest of whales.

and expose it to searing heat or bitter cold, the challenge to survival has produced the greatest diversity of life. The rate of evolution is slower the deeper one goes into the ocean, because uniform conditions do not promote selection and because the lower temperatures cause chemical reactions to occur more slowly. The ocean shields its creatures from cosmic rays which can produce mutations, so it seems likely that cosmic radiation is unimportant in the sea when compared to the natural mutation rate provided by the thermal agitation of matter. We find in the oceans living fossils, forms of life that have not changed for millions of years. Among these are *coelacanths*,

perhaps the link between fish and land vertebrates, and the shellfish, *Hutchinsoniella*, living in Long Island mud on the doorstep of the most modern city in the world and relating the ancient fossil *trilobites* to the horseshoe crabs. As we find better ways to observe and collect in the ocean, we will find many more forms unchanged through ages on lower rungs of the ladder of evolution.

One theory of the origin of life is that ultraviolet light and lightning transformed gases into more complicated compounds, the building blocks for life that gathered in the sea. Over two and one-half billion years ago, the first living cells reproduced and gradually developed into marine plants and boneless animals; the first fish came less than half a billion years ago. During this time, plants began to grow on land, providing an environment for the sea animals which crawled out and pioneered the land. From these early forms came the amphibians, reptiles,

Most sea-dwelling animals have a few relatives which now live in fresh-water or on land. These sea-urchins, however, and their relatives, the starfishes, sea cucumbers, and sand dollars, are found only in salt water.

mammals and birds that lived out of water.

Only a million years ago men came. Even our ears developed from gill slits and our blood still has the same proportion of salt as in sea water, though more diluted. All land animals once had ancestors living in the sea. We learn this time table from the fossils in rocks and sediments; but in our ladder of evolution there are many missing rungs. Because conditions in the sea bottom have changed less than on land, there is more chance of finding missing ancient types of life preserved there.

Floating at or near the surface of the sea is a blanket of billions of tiny plants, microscopic phytoplankton, that make up the green pastures of the sea—the food for all sea animals.

Plant plankton utilize the inorganic gases, water, and minerals, but must have energy of sunlight to function. So the little plants grow only in the upper sunlit waters.

There are tiny animals, zooplankton, in the surface blanket, too. They feed on the fiber plankton and are fed on, in turn, by grazing fish, like herring and mackerel. Even the largest of all living animals, the blue whale, lives on tiny shrimp. In the middle layers of the sea where light does not penetrate, there are no plants so the fish eat either the plankton animals that sink down or other fish.

Even at the bottom of the sea, fish live that have adapted to the darkness and to preying on other fish for their food. They wear dark colors and so hide from others that would eat them. Some have adapted in extraordinary ways, like the angler fish whose top fin has grown into a fishing rod and line with a luminous lure on the end. One angler fish, *Melanocutus Johnsoni*, has hinged jaws like a boa constrictor and can swallow a fish many times his own size. Other bottom fish have developed their fins and tails into long legs, and sea spiders are found nearly two miles down on the bottom of the sea. There are also rooted animals that feed, without moving, on the rain of zooplankton from the surface. In the darkness of the deep, fish have adapted either by becoming blind, or by developing huge eyes, or by making their own light which they flash on and off. Some make sounds and listen for the echo from the bottom or from their prey.

Beneath a mile and a half of water, a sea spider steps lightly along the ocean bottom. This remarkable photograph was taken by a specially designed automatic camera carrying its own electronic light source. The camera was lowered from the Research vessel Eltanin *near South Orkney Island, in the Scotia Sea.*

A group of Snares Island Penguins, New Zealand.

On the edge of the sea, there are animals that live half in and half out of water. Penguins live where there is no fresh water, but they desalinize sea water by exuding salt from their noses. Seals and walruses were once land animals and still bear their young on land, but spend most of their time in the sea, where they get their food. Whales and dolphins (mammals like ourselves) were once land animals that returned to the sea.

Like an iceberg, only part of a walrus' huge bulk shows above the surface. A large male will weigh almost a ton and a half. Like seals, walruses come to land to give birth to their young but spend most of their lives in the water.

A dredge-net (top of picture) has just brought up a haul of various bottom-dwelling snails and clams. A worker sorts out the edible species.

CONSERVING LIFE IN THE SEA

Until recently, the worst threat to the natural balance of the ocean community was the possible extinction of certain marine animals. Generally those threatened are edible species that travel in schools or sea mammals that are easy to slaughter. Eighty per cent of all fur seals of the world are born on their land home in the tiny Pribilof Islands in the Bering Sea. When the islands were discovered two hundred years ago, there were two and one-half million seals there, but by the turn of our century killing on land and wasteful slaughter at sea had eliminated sixteen out of every seventeen seals! The herd was almost extinct. Fortunately, with a series of international agreements to protect it, the herd has now grown back to one and one-half million. The International Agreement on Whaling limits the length of the whaling season, the number of whales, the minimum size, and protects nursing mothers, calves, Right whales and Pacific Grey whales. But even with this agreement, there is still a danger that whales may disappear from the seas.

Even such ordinary fish as Pacific halibut and tropical tuna have now reached the point where the amount of fish taken is close to the amount which will naturally grow back. The maximum sustainable yield for Eastern Pacific halibut is about seventy-five million pounds annually, and the catch is about the same. Of course, it is hard to make a census of a particular species of fish in the sea, but fishing must be done on the basis of "borrowing from nature instead of robbing her." In the case of tropical tuna, the Inter-American Commission estimates an annual sustained catch of a little less than 100,000 tons. Two hundred ordinary tuna boats can hook this in half a year. In 1961, intensive unregulated fishing took more than this amount. If this goes on, tuna will be steadily depleted. Furthermore, it is not sensible for the fishermen as they have to fish harder to catch less.

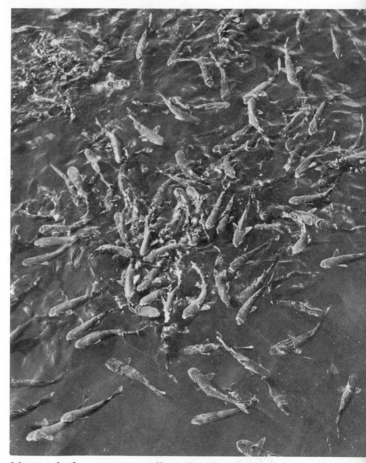

Most of the commercially-valuable food fishes occur in schools like this group of mullet. These fish are all about the same size indicating that they were hatched the same year.

This net-haul of shrimp is an example of the productivity of the sea. This productivity will be increased as men find ways to "farm" the sea.

These are just a few examples to show what we do to the sea by over-fishing. Intensive fishing is carried on by the Russians off Nova Scotia, using a 17,500 ton mother vessel with twenty smaller fishing vessels that pour fish into her holds. As soon as she has about six thousand tons of fish, she rushes to shore leaving the little vessels to go on fishing. She discharges the cargo and comes back for more. This kind of organized, intensive fishing promises to increase in the future.

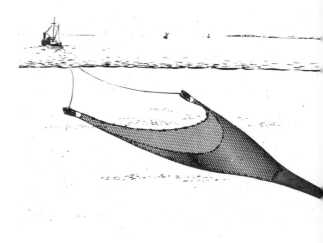

This diagram of a shrimp boat or "trawler" shows the type of net, known as a trawl, used to catch shrimp.

COMPETITIVE USES
OF THE SEASHORE

The continental shelves, bays, estuaries, and shorelines are the nurseries, or spawning grounds, for many fish and shellfish. They are also the areas most intensively fished and most vulnerable because of the ease of taking fish from them. Yet it is in these very parts of the ocean waters (most important for some of the life in the sea) that pollution by man is growing to alarming proportions.

Along the seashore, engineers build concrete embankments to prevent the shifting of sand or the erosion of "valuable land." Promoters fill estuarian waters to make shoreline property. What semi-enclosed waters are left are often fouled by industrial activity, and the man-made locks and dams often plug up the already insufficient "flushing" so the pollution cannot drain into the open ocean. Even man's thirst for fresh water affects the edges of the sea. The needs of fresh water will soon be such that not a drop from the rivers will flow into the sea. Thus, the natural supply of dissolved salts and sand carried down by the rivers will be cut off. If the dissolved salts from land are prevented from going into the sea, we may be tampering with nature's balance. The two billion tons of salt that are carried into the sea each year are only one millionth of the total salt in the sea. Cutting this off completely might seem to be an effect measurable only over a million years, but

we don't know. Salts do not just stay in the sea. They have varying "residence times." Some are taken up in the body skeletons of the sea animals that sink to the bottom to be lost in the sediments. We have an inkling that certain trace elements of salt in minute concentrations affect the growth of fish. Perhaps cutting off the supply may have a profound effect on sea life. On the positive side, we may be able to introduce trace elements and promote growth of fish.

Man's interference with the sand, however, is also serious. California beaches are already being lost. Beaches are the result of a dynamic equilibrium of sand brought down by the rivers, "residing" in the beaches for a while, but then continuing its journey to be lost in the deep sea. When the rivers no longer flow, this sand is not replenished. Perhaps we'll have to dredge it up from the sea bottom and put it back to maintain the beaches.

Do you recognize the curious conflict between the land, water and seashore conservationists? We try to fight erosion of the land. If this were done perfectly, there would be no sand in river water. We try to conserve fresh water. If this were done perfectly, all water would return to the sea through many reused cycles of transpiration, evaporation into the air, then falling as rain back into the ocean. But then, what would happen to our beaches?

Seashores are subjected to the eroding forces of wind and waves and have always been changeable. Although built to stabilize the shore, sea walls and dikes sometimes cause changes in water currents and may actually increase erosion. Here the Pacific Ocean encroaches on a row of beach houses.

POLLUTION

The ocean has been used as a garbage dump probably as long as man has been on earth. And as long as the wastes were natural organic refuse, not much harm was done. In fact, it could be argued that perhaps these wastes fertilized and possibly added to the productivity of the sea. But now all kinds of new inorganic chemicals and poisons are being poured into the oceans.

Fifty-two million people live within a fifty-mile belt along the coast of the continental United States. This coastal belt, representing about eight per cent of the total land area of the United States, contains 29 per cent of our population and a vast industrial complex. Both the population and the industrial development in this coastal region have been increasing at about 2.5 per cent per year, with no indication of a reversal in this upward trend. We have always used the adjacent marine environment as a receiver of unwanted municipal and industrial waste products. The increase in population density is causing a shift from individual septic systems to large-scale sewage networks. Many of these systems discharge treated or partially-treated effluent directly into coastal embayments and estuaries or through outfalls into open coastal waters. As a result of this trend, the use of marine environment as a dump of waste components is increasing at a much faster rate than the population growth of the coastal region.

There are many kinds of pollution of the edges of the sea. If you have gummed up your feet or shoes with that black, tarry oil on the beach, you became annoyed; but how much more serious this is to the organisms that live in the sea! This oil comes from washing out oil tankers at sea or from discharging oily water ballast from fuel tanks of cargo vessels. When covered with oil, lobsters do not breed, sea birds can neither swim nor fly, fish cannot be washed and eaten and, even if, as they say, clams *can* live in oil polluted water, who wants to eat an oily clam? Where the ducks winter, more may be killed by oil than by hunters. Oil can change the migration routes of fish and keep them away from their breeding grounds.

The excuse for not worrying too much about the sea as a garbage dump is that it is so large that it can dilute almost anything. The fallacy in this is that sea organisms selectively concentrate certain poisons and wastes. Shellfish do this naturally when they are exposed to the dinoflagellate "red tide." With twenty million pounds of DDT used on our land per year, we each have accumulated (because it is hard to metabolize) one gram of DDT, or twelve parts per million, in the fat of our own bodies. There was a report that fifty parts per million of DDT have been found in fish fifty miles offshore. Biologists do not know how the fish acquired this, but it dramatizes future dangers.

When atomic energy is produced, radioactive waste products accumulate. These dangerous materials must be disposed of without contaminating our environment. Its deck lined with containers of deadly radioactive waste, a vessel puts out towards the deepest part of the sea, there to unload its cargo. We may find at a future date that even these remote dumping grounds were not safe.

Because of the size and volume of the oceans, man has not until recently been able to ruin the sea as much as he has the land by deforestation, overgrazing and consequent erosion. But now he has more powerful tools, such as atomic explosions, at his disposal. With these and well-meaning, short-sighted efforts to "control" the sea, he has now within his grasp the power to do irreparable harm. When he first was faced with a new kind of waste, atomic waste, it was natural that he should immediately think of the sea as the solution to his problem. At first, radioactive wastes were dumped in concrete-covered steel drums in fairly shallow waters, but even such containers can leak or be broken by accident. So, next he sought deep parts of the sea where the water was dead still, so that even if a leak occurred, the wastes would not be stirred into the rest of the sea. Also, he looked for places in the ocean where the sedimentation rates were high so that, hopefully, by the time the container deteriorated, it would be covered by a layer of natural sediments.

None of these attempts are even steps toward an ultimate solution. Animals, even in the still waters of the deep, may concentrate the radioactivity. Within the long half-lifetimes of some of the radioactive materials, man may need to mine, stir, or otherwise disturb the seabottom, or it might be disturbed by earthquakes which would cause the containers to break apart.

The major sources of radioactive materials put into the sea have been from nuclear installations on rivers. Radioactivity in dissolved or suspended material is carried down by the river water used for cooling. The Columbia River carries off radioactivity contributed by the plant at Hanford at a rate of about one thousand curies a day. Even though the concentrations in the Columbia River water are low enough so that the water is drinkable, radioactivity may be reconcentrated by marine organisms.

Advocates of "peaceful uses" of atomic explosives propose to use nuclear bombs to blast out a harbor, to create a new Panama Canal and to do other "exciting" plastic surgery on the face of the earth. They maintain that these are "clean" nuclear explosions. But how clean is clean? There is a simple progression of events that scientists should always bear in mind when dealing with the environment. It is simply this: observation, understanding, prediction and then control. In the sea in relation to its total ecology, we do not even yet have the observational knowledge on which to base a proper understanding. Certainly we should not attempt large scale control before we can predict what the results of this control will be.

TAKING A CENSUS IN THE SEA

Before we can predict and control, we must observe and understand. The first thing we should do about the sea is a survey of the oceans designed to give us the necessary observations toward an understanding of the life cycles in them.

In order to plan to take as much, but not more, than the sea can grow in a sustained fashion, we need a census or inventory of the things we take from the sea. Fishery scientists have made an excellent beginning at a census for halibut, whales and tuna. Usually, this involves some form of tag attached to the fish. When you take a census of people, you can do it at one time and eliminate the effects of migrations; but, in taking a census of the ocean of those larger animals that migrate widely, counting them involves a knowledge of where they go. Space satellites with their world-wide line of sight can help in studying these migrations. Tuna, salmon, whales and such can be tagged with tiny radio transmitters. These will not bother them because the devices can be made "weightless" in sea water. They can be used only on organisms that come to the surface. Their tiny radio voices can be picked up by orbiting satellites and relayed back to earth to tell us just where the different tagged species were.

We need more research so that we may understand the total ecology of the oceans; how shifting sands affect marine life; how organisms concentrate certain substances selectively; how fast the stirring of the ocean is. We must find out how fast pollution may be distributed and how stirring brings up the necessary nutrients to the lighted zone where they can be used in a biologically productive manner. We must learn to use the sea so that subsequent generations can reuse it. For example, we already know that all wastes need not be prohibited from the sea. We know that if they are put in selectively and intelligently, not just in the cheapest way possible, they could do good instead of harm. Organic wastes at the proper dilution in the upper lighted waters of the sea could be the "fertilizers" for life there. Waste heat discharged lower down could cause nutrient-rich lower water to be brought up to the surface layers where the nutrients would do the most good.

What Steps Should be Taken Toward Conservation in the Sea

Until we know more about the total ecology of the seas from our observations and studies of them, we should have widespread areas where we do not tamper with the natural balance. But with the oceans belonging to no one person, no one nation, but to all, *who* is responsbile and can take the initiative in their conservation? The only answer is all of us — whether it be by concerted action in the fringes of our own territorial waters or by international agreements for the open sea.

A skin diver enjoying the beautiful formations of several different types of coral.

Protecting Our Own Watery Backyard

The most vulnerable areas of marine life are on the fringes of the seas. Here, sport fishermen may be an even greater menace than commercial fishermen. The sport fisherman will often, without regard to cost, get chemical lures, fish calls, or underwater guns which leave the poor fish no chance at all. Furthermore, he often goes after a species he prefers and threatens its extinction. People could still enjoy the sea and the life in it, but in a constructive way by underwater photography and skin diving, or by fish lists and counts which would assist in the vast task of taking the census of the sea.

Ocean Tanks and Aquariums

Because the will to conserve develops with understanding and appreciation of the life in the sea, we need more good aquariums where people can gain an appreciation and an interest in the marvelous cycles of the sealife. TV aquariums can even bring the sea to the center of a great continent. No longer will it be necessary to have oceanographic institutions only on the seashore. Land is just a little island—the sea-shore is accessible to everyone. Ocean parks, of which we have a few in the United States, contribute to this enjoyable enlightenment and offer a measure of protection. But just as the national parks of land perform one function, and the wilderness areas another, so ocean parks alone cannot adequately do the job of preserving the natural balance of the sea. We also need more thoroughly protected waters.

TV aquariums will make it possible for people living all over a great continent to enjoy the profusion of life in the sea.

Ocean Wilderness

The magnificent wilderness areas on land which are being set aside in the United States do only half the job. We must extend the concept of wilderness areas so that we will have some that include estuaries, seashores, enclosed bodies of water and open sea, right out to our territorial limits.

We must do this soon or there won't be a foot of the United States seashore that isn't concreted up with levees, docks and buildings forming a continuous Coney Island — Atlantic City — Miami complex from the northern end of Maine right around to Seattle. But national wilderness areas of the sea are just the first step. We must further extend the concept to international oceanic wildernesses. Fortunately, there still remain some uninhabited islands in the oceans and these could be the start. Nightingale and Inaccessible in the Tristan da Cunha group in the south Atlantic come to mind. There are many other islands in various parts of the world ocean which could be the centers of wilderness areas.

The diving suit with its heavy copper helmet was invented by August Siebe and has been in continuous use for nearly 150 years. A diver's freedom is restricted because of its weight and surface connected air hose.

MAN IN THE SEA

Going Deep into the Sea

It is only in the last few years that we have begun to go down into the ocean to see things for ourselves. Up to that time, our knowledge came from the gatherings of nets operated from surface vessels like blind men making butterfly collections. Vehicles to take us deep down into the sea were not available and so we concentrated on developing instruments for measuring its characteristics from the surface.

Diving suits, supplied with air through hoses from the surface, were used for a long time. But the hoses were a nuisance when moving around. For almost a hundred years, men have been working on the idea of a self-contained breathing apparatus that a skin diver could carry. In 1943, two French scientists, Jacques-Yves Cousteau and Emile Gagnan, perfected underwater breathing by inventing the aqualung. After that, by carrying air in bottles on their backs, men could explore the shallow edges of the sea. Skin diving enables almost anyone to see the profusion of life in the shallow edges of the sea. But to reach some sunken ships and underwater landmarks, it was clearly worthwhile to dive deeper.

To do that, though, man needed a hard shield about him. The pressure in some places he wanted to visit would be equal to seven tons per square inch.

Since the invention of the aqualung in 1943 by two French scientists, man has had great freedom to explore the shallow edges of the ocean. Here a diver enters the shark-proof "porch" of an early "sealab," two hundred feet down in the Atlantic.

In 1930, Dr. William Beebe, a famous naturalist, who had already explored tropical jungles, decided to go down and see the life in the depths of the ocean. He built his bathysphere four and one half feet in diameter of inch and one-half thick steel weighing two tons. It had heavy quartz windows through which he could observe and photograph. The bathysphere carried its own oxygen, was lowered by a strong steel cable from a crane on the mother ship and had telephone and electric current lines connecting to it. In the bathysphere, Dr. Beebe went down to the record depth of over half a mile in the 1930's.

The pioneer bathyscaph Trieste, *which carried two men 35,800 feet down into the sea and back. The pressure-proof sphere which housed the scientists projects beneath the hull. The* Trieste *was much more successful than the earlier non-mobile bathysphere, but for work at intermediate depths it has been superseded by more versatile craft.*

The lines and connections to the mother ship were dangerous and cumbersome and a Swiss scientist, Dr. Auguste Piccard, conceived the idea of freeing the sphere which housed the men and supporting it by a buoyant hull — the hull was filled with lighter-than-water gasoline. Weights on the bathyscaph carried it down and were released when it was desired to rise to the surface again. The bathyscaph carried its own power to light lights, work instruments and was freed from the mother ship.

Though the bathyscaph could go up and down like an undersea balloon, its two small propellers gave it very little maneuverability horizontally. In the bathyscaph, *Trieste,* the son of the inventor, Jacques Piccard, and Lt. Don Walsh of the United States Navy, went down nearly 36,000 feet to the bottom of a Pacific Ocean trench in 1960.

PACIFIC OCEAN

GUAM

{ CHALLENGER DEEP 35,800 FEET

Many improvements in design and structure have been made on **Trieste II** *for better maneuverability underwater and greater strength and stability while being towed on the surface.*

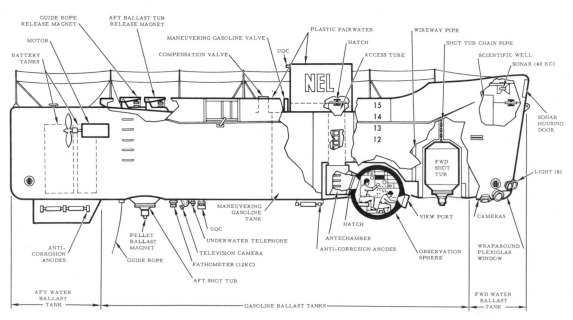

GUIDE ROPE
RELEASE MAGNET

AFT BALLAST TUB
RELEASE MAGNET

MOTOR

MANEUVERING GASOLINE VALVE

BATTERY
TANKS

COMPENSATION VALVE

UQC

PLASTIC FAIRWATER

HATCH

ACCESS TUBE

WIREWAY PIPE

SHOT TUB CHAIN PIPE

SCIENTIFIC WELL

SONAR (40 KC)

NEL

15
14
13
12

FWD
SHOT
TUB

SONAR
HOUSING
DOOR

LIGHT (8)

MANEUVERING
GASOLINE
TANK

HATCH

VIEW PORT

CAMERAS

UQC

ANTECHAMBER

ANTI-
CORROSION
ANODES

PELLET
BALLAST
MAGNET

UNDERWATER TELEPHONE

ANTI-CORROSION ANODES

OBSERVATION
SPHERE

WRAPAROUND
PLEXIGLAS
WINDOW

TELEVISION CAMERA

GUIDE ROPE

FATHOMETER (12KC)

AFT SHOT TUB

AFT WATER
BALLAST
TANK

GASOLINE BALLAST TANKS

FWD WATER
BALLAST
TANK

Cutaway drawing of **Trieste II.**

Next to come were more maneuverable undersea exploring craft and one of the first was a diving jet-propelled saucer-like submarine which would carry two men to moderate depths, move about and even pick up specimens that the men saw through its plexiglass eyes.

This is the original "diving saucer," the pioneer "mesoscaph" or medium-depth diving craft. It has made hundreds of dives and serves as a prototype for most subsequent submersibles.

Another view of the Diving Saucer being lifted out of the water after completing a dive. This vehicle propelled by 2 rotatable water jets is extremely maneuverable and carries 2 men to a depth of 1000 feet.

A cross section view of the Diving Saucer.

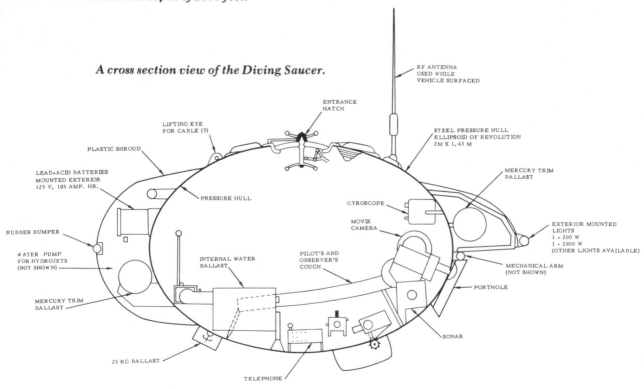

RF ANTENNA
USED WHILE
VEHICLE SURFACED

ENTRANCE
HATCH

LIFTING EYE
FOR CABLE (3)

STEEL PRESSURE HULL
ELLIPSOID OF REVOLUTION
2M X 1.43 M

PLASTIC SHROUD

LEAD-ACID BATTERIES
MOUNTED EXTERIOR
125 V, 105 AMP. HR.

MERCURY TRIM
BALLAST

PRESSURE HULL

GYROSCOPE

MOVIE
CAMERA

EXTERIOR MOUNTED
LIGHTS
1 - 200 W
1 - 2800 W
(OTHER LIGHTS AVAILABLE)

RUBBER BUMPER

WATER PUMP
FOR HYDROJETS
(NOT SHOWN)

INTERNAL WATER
BALLAST

PILOT'S AND
OBSERVER'S
COUCH

MECHANICAL ARM
(NOT SHOWN)

PORTHOLE

MERCURY TRIM
BALLAST

SONAR

25 KG BALLAST

TELEPHONE

76

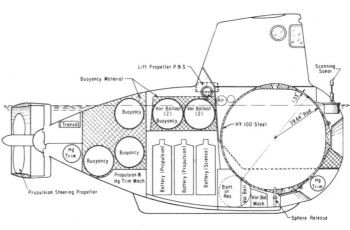

The Alvin built for the Woods Hole Oceanographic Institution, can carry two men down to 6,000 feet. It is an example of the many highly-maneuverable, mid-range submersibles now being built.

This diagram of the Alvin shows the thick-walled pressure-proof personnel sphere which is a fundamental part of almost all of the deep-diving craft.

Since then, all sorts and sizes of deep-diving submarines have been developed. The deep-diving, manned vehicles are like lobsters, able to go up and down, move horizontally in the water in any depth and crawl along the bottom. Some have mechanical arms like claws, remotely controlled by the man in the pressure-tight shell. The man's eyes are extended by a television circuit with the pickup on the end of the controllable hand. More flexible than our own eyes, it can turn in any direction and present what it sees on a screen to the man inside. If it sees a rock of interest, the claw-like hands can take an underwater geologist's hammer and collect the specimen. If it sees a fish, it can collect it with a net. If it sees ripples and sediments, it can photograph and measure them. Directed by the knowledge and experience of the investigator inside the cabin, it can multiply many times over the amount of information that could be secured by instruments alone.

This close-up photo shows the Alvin's mechanical claw which can be operated from within the pressure-proof personnel sphere.

*The **Star II** is one of a series of deep-diving craft built by United States' industries.*

When we descend to these depths, we have to protect ourselves from the tremendous external pressures by a strong, water-tight cabin which maintains our normal air pressure of fifteen pounds per square inch inside. Animals that have adapted themselves to the darkness of the depths and the pressure of seven miles of sea water on top of them die when caught by chance in trawls operated from the surface because now, when they are brought to the surface, the change in pressure kills them. But they can be collected and placed in a strong container which will keep them at their accustomed pressure, temperature and darkness while they are brought to the surface alive to be studied in oceanariums specially designed to reproduce the physical conditions under which they live and in which they may reproduce themselves.

These small deep-water bathyscaphs are launched from and return to a mother ship. The mother ships are surface vessels now, but later we may see large, very-deep-water submarines acting as bases for the small, inquisitive, manned bathyscaphs which would scatter to collect the data and return to report to her from time to time. These new means of

CUTAWAY OF STAR II

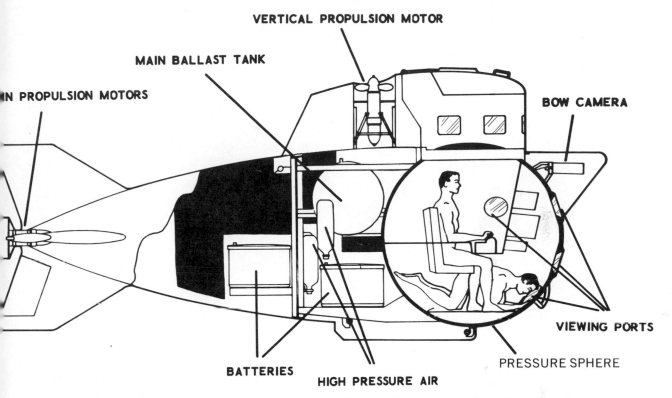

VERTICAL PROPULSION MOTOR

MAIN BALLAST TANK

N PROPULSION MOTORS

BOW CAMERA

VIEWING PORTS

PRESSURE SPHERE

BATTERIES

HIGH PRESSURE AIR

*This cutaway drawing shows that the **Star II** is built around a pressure sphere. The smooth, trim hull around the ballast tanks and batteries is not watertight and does not have to withstand great pressures.*

gathering data will lead to world-wide maps of the ocean's plant, animal and total biological life. We do not have these yet, and neither have our aquariums grown to the size where, under controlled conditions that we can observe, we can study the interactions of total communities of ocean life. But we will have huge oceanariums where we can learn why organisms and fish perform migrations, vertical and horizontal; whether they navigate celestially as the birds perhaps do; how creatures in the darkest recesses seven miles down generate their own lights within their bodies; and how they withstand the tremendous pressures. We are just beginning to have the tools and materials to build these immense facilities, and whether we will take large samples of the ocean and place them in plastic tanks on land where we can control temperature, pressure, nutrients and other conditions, or whether we will build plastic houses at the bottom of the sea so that we can observe denizens at home, I do not know. I expect we will probably do both when we decide seriously to engineer the oceans and develop ocean agriculture.

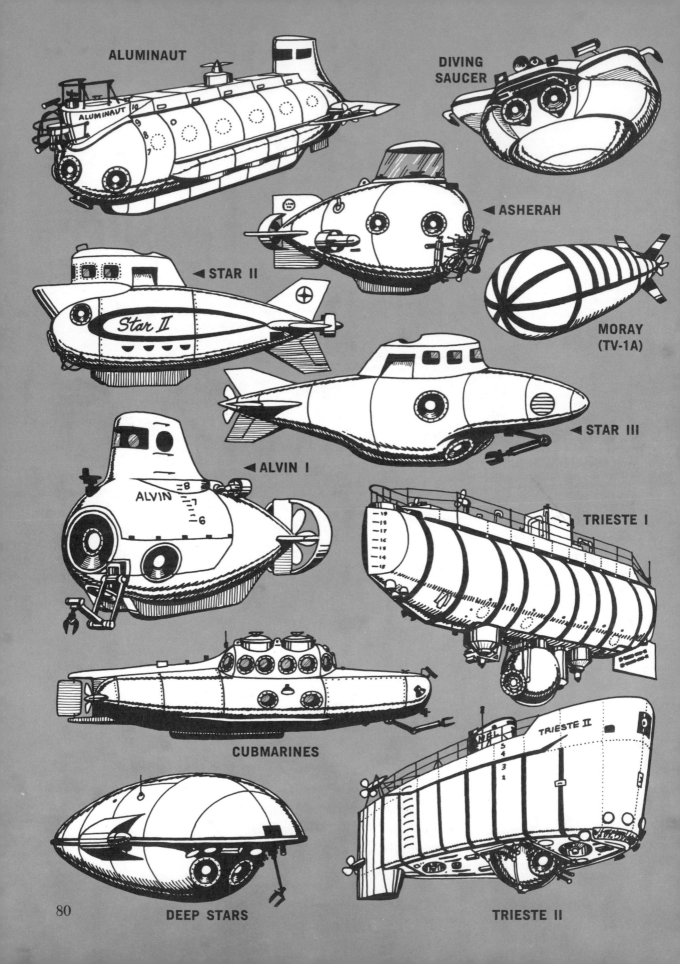

ALUMINAUT

ALUMINAUT

DIVING
SAUCER

◀ ASHERAH

◀ STAR II

Star II

MORAY
(TV-1A)

◀ STAR III

◀ ALVIN I

ALVIN

TRIESTE I

CUBMARINES

TRIESTE II

80

DEEP STARS

TRIESTE II

MANNED RESEARCH SUBMERSIBLES

NAME	CREW	MAXIMUM DEPTH IN FEET	SPEED IN KNOTS	PAYLOAD IN POUNDS	MAXIMUM HOURS UNDERSEA
ALUMINAUT	3 + 4 OBSERVERS	15,000	4	6,000	72
ALVIN I	1 + 1 OBSERVER	6,000	4	1,200	24
ASHERAH	2	600	4	250	24
CUBMARINE PC3A	2	300	4	750	20
CUBMARINE PC3B	2	600	4	950	20
CUBMARINE PLC4	2 + 2 DIVERS	1,500	4	1,500	36
DEEP STAR 2,000	2 + 1 OBSERVER	2,000	4	1,000	48
DEEP STAR 4,000	2 + 1 OBSERVER	4,000	3	100 MINIMUM	48
DEEP STAR 13,000	2 + 1 OBSERVER	13,000	3	100 MINIMUM	48
DEEP STAR 20,000	2 + 1 OBSERVER	20,000	3	100 MINIMUM	48
DIVING SAUCER	1 + 1 OBSERVER	1,000	1	100 MINIMUM	24
MORAY (TV-1A)	2	6,000	15	200	24
STAR I	1	200	1	200	18
STAR II	2	600	4	250	24
STAR III	2	2,000	4	1,000	24
TRIESTE I	1 + 1 OBSERVER	36,000	2	20,000	24
TRIESTE II	1 + 2 OBSERVERS	36,000	4	20,000	24

An underwater view of a small two-man submarine which is designed primarily for exploration of relatively shallow waters to 600 feet.

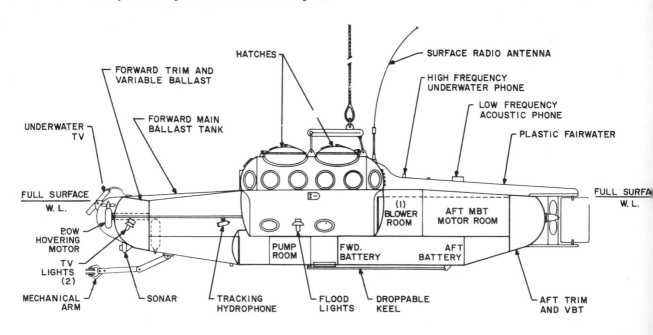

Cutaway drawing of the **Perry Cubmarine PC3B.**

OCEAN ENGINEERING

From time to time we give names to assemblages of our different scientific disciplines for the reason that they apply to and suit our principal current preoccupations. So, polar science is the science relating to the Arctic and Antarctic. Space science is all science dealing with space. Similarly, oceanography and marine science comprise the work of any scientist in any discipline who chooses to use the sea as focus for his endeavors.

What is ocean engineering? In engineering the qualifying nouns become more meaningful. The engineering problems of the polar regions are quite special and unique. How do you get rid of sewage when everything is frozen? How do you build foundations that sink in permafrost? How do you build structures in slowly flowing ice? Engineering for space, too, has its special problems. Metals can cold-weld themselves together in the vacuum of space. Special lubricants are needed, and vacuum tubes may not need an outside cover. So it is in ocean engineering. Materials behave quite differently at the seven-ton-per-square-inch pressures encountered in the abyss. Structures must be built to resist the onslaught of marine borers and other living organisms that attack them, and they must withstand entirely different catastrophic forces—earthquakes, currents, wave forces and underwater landslides.

We must recall that where science aims at finding out enough about our environment to describe it and then to find common truths, engineering sets about with express plans and design to alter and use the environment. The uses and controls that are found acceptable—those that society wants or can learn to want—industries apply so that they can be used by as many people as possible.

There are two kinds of ocean engineering: there is that kind that has gone on for centuries like the building of ships to get from one point of land to another and the building of dikes to keep the sea from encroaching on the land. But these are merely in support of peripheral activities of land-based and oriented people—not *using* the sea but *withstanding* its abuse of the land. There is another kind of ocean engineering, and that is the ocean engineering which must come about when we decide intentionally to master our oceans with the ultimate objectives of using them, occupying them and enjoying them.

The **Perry Cubmarine** *after surfacing from a dive; note the several viewing ports for excellent underwater observation.*

When you occupy a place, whether it be an enemy country, uninhabited polar or desert wastes, the moon, the planets, or the depths of the sea, you need five basic things for people to live: a way to get there and back, shelter while you're there, power, water and food.

Of course, it's not necessary to occupy the ocean right now. We can choose freely to expend part of our efforts and apply our marine, scientific and oceanographic knowledge toward the peaceful exploitation and colonization of the sea. When we decide to occupy the ocean then we no longer are merely predicting the future; we are inventing the future.

Transportation, shelter, power, water and food — to these five basic needs for the living on earth must be added a sixth for the habitation of the sea. We can live quite a while without food and water, but you could not have read the last few sentences without breathing. An important project in ocean engineering is the medical research being done on breathing at high pressures. At the present time men are spending weeks below hundreds of feet of

The Aluminaut, *designed to go down to 15,000 feet differs from all of the other deep-submersibles in that the personnel are carried in a long, pressure-proof cylinder rather than a ball. Its crew of three can move about freely in its roomy interior, protected by aluminum walls six inches thick.*

This view of the **Aluminaut** *submersed shows the viewing ports in its rounded nose. Special underwater cameras mounted on the bow are protected by a framework of stout tubing.*

water breathing mixtures, mostly of inert helium, with just the right small percentage of oxygen so that at those depths it's compressed to about the oxygen pressure in the normal atmosphere. Ocean medicine has found that helium does not give the narcotic effect "rapture of the deep" that comes from the great solubility of nitrogen in fatty nerve cells. Ocean medicine, by studying decompression, is beginning to overcome the dangers when the aquanaut comes up and reduces his pressure too quickly. If he does, the gases expand in bubbles that block arteries, attack joints and give him the fatal "bends."

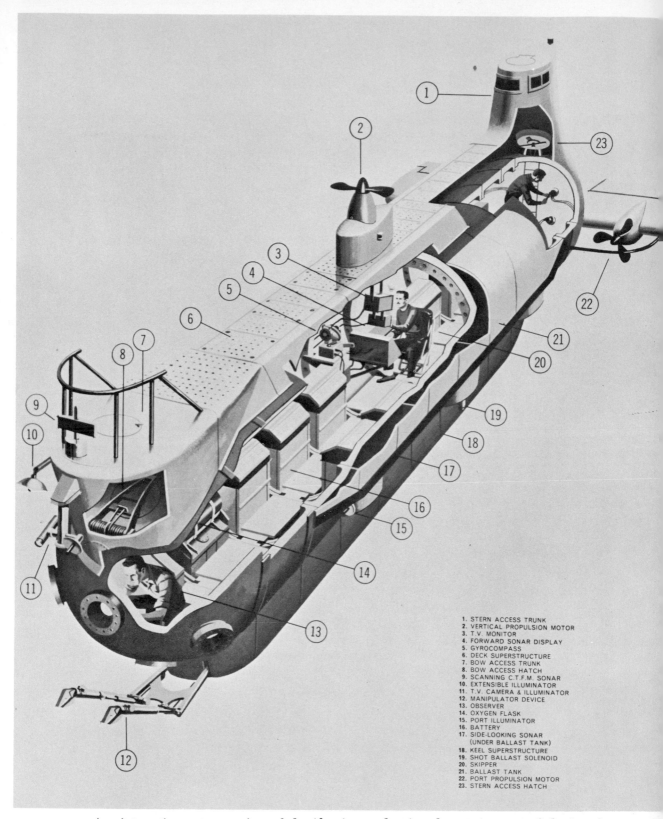

1. STERN ACCESS TRUNK
2. VERTICAL PROPULSION MOTOR
3. T.V. MONITOR
4. FORWARD SONAR DISPLAY
5. GYROCOMPASS
6. DECK SUPERSTRUCTURE
7. BOW ACCESS TRUNK
8. BOW ACCESS HATCH
9. SCANNING C.T.F.M. SONAR
10. EXTENSIBLE ILLUMINATOR
11. T.V. CAMERA & ILLUMINATOR
12. MANIPULATOR DEVICE
13. OBSERVER
14. OXYGEN FLASK
15. PORT ILLUMINATOR
16. BATTERY
17. SIDE-LOOKING SONAR
    (UNDER BALLAST TANK)
18. KEEL SUPERSTRUCTURE
19. SHOT BALLAST SOLENOID
20. SKIPPER
21. BALLAST TANK
22. PORT PROPULSION MOTOR
23. STERN ACCESS HATCH

An interesting cutaway view of the Aluminaut, *showing the spaciousness of the interior and its unique construction.*

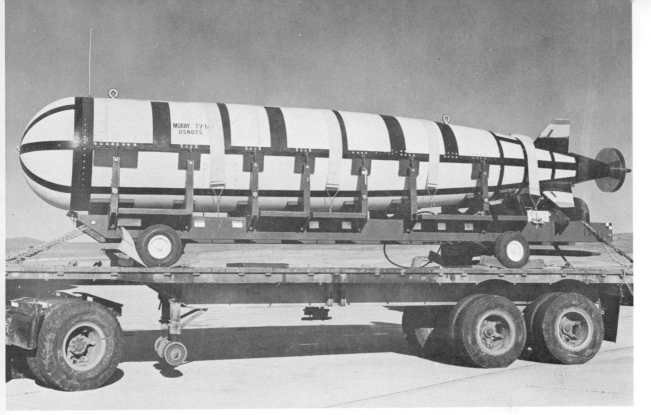

The Moray (TV-1A) is another interesting approach to the design of deep-sea research vehicles, carries two men to 6,000 feet and has no viewing ports, using 2 TV cameras instead.

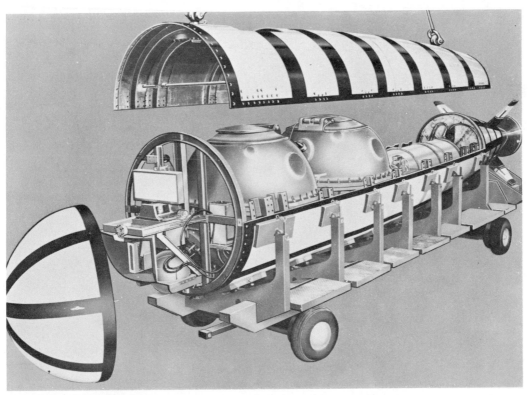

The outside fiberglas hull has been removed to show the two cast aluminum, bolted spheres in which the crew rides.

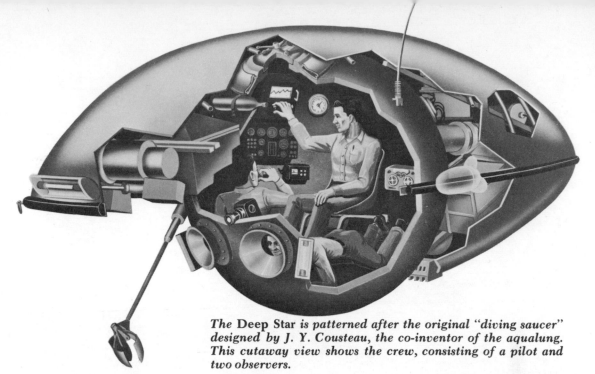

The Deep Star is patterned after the original "diving saucer" designed by J. Y. Cousteau, the co-inventor of the aqualung. This cutaway view shows the crew, consisting of a pilot and two observers.

Under experimental conditions mice and other small mammals have been able to survive under water by breathing water, actually inhaling and exhaling the liquid. This may point to engineering developments of the future. Man may yet qualify as an *aquatic mammal*.

Of the other five basics, three deal mainly with physical engineering — the provision of new surface and submarine vehicles, structures under the sea, and power generators. Ocean engineering also includes food and water — fishing, fish farming, hybridizing marine plants, and even water divining in the sea — the search for undersea fresh water springs. In the meantime, we can, of course, desalt sea water, but this is a clumsy interim method.

Ocean engineers must face problems quite different from engineering experiences on land. Electrolysis dictates a different choice of metals. The mechanical stresses of current, waves and undersea earthquakes are quite different from their counterparts on land. Marine life can bore,

excavate and undermine undersea structures; and other oganisms can create unwanted noise. So biological engineering is a necessary aid even to the physical engineering in the oceans. Biological engineering will play a far greater part in the oceans than it has in the physical engineering of the land. I do not mean to imply that the ocean engineer must be any more competent than the most competent land engineers; but he must be able to combine the basic sciences and, even more important, he needs a different focus. The focus of the land engineer is to prevent the encroachment of the sea, to concrete up coastlines, to fill estuaries for land habitations. The ocean engineer will consider it more important that beaches and estuaries be retained, or even that new ones be built, because they are the habitat of many valuable shellfish and the nursery of many fish of the deep sea.

For many years a gap existed between the scientists and oceanographers who made such great strides

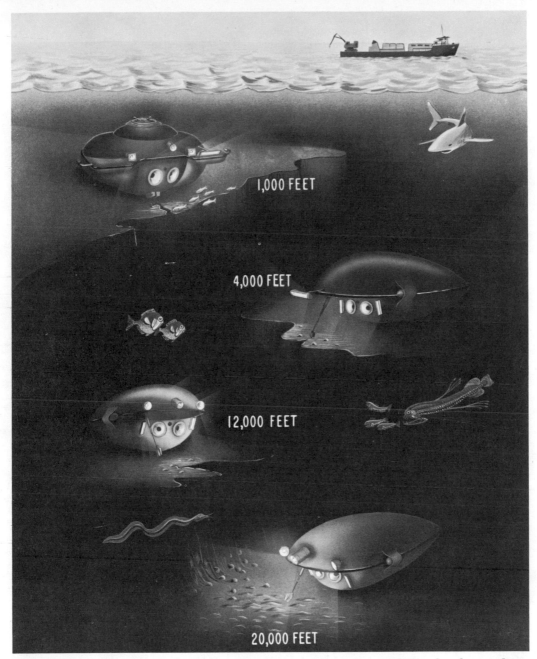

Deep Stars *of different capabilities are now being built, the largest being fitted to go down to 20,000 feet.*

in describing and understanding the ocean environment — its shores, its bottom, its physical and living contents — and the fishermen, navigators, sea captains and sailors who use the sea. Ocean engineering will fill the gap, pull out many useful scientific findings and translate them into better ways of using the sea.

Up to now, the main uses of the sea were for surface ships and fishing. Surface ships operate at the worst possible level — on the surface of the sea. At this interface, they are plagued by wind, waves and ice. If they would go a little way up or a little way down, they would be better off.

Sealab *is a name applied to a series of projects of the U. S. Navy in which divers have lived on the ocean floor for several weeks at a time, sleeping and eating in submerged, pressurized home bases like that in the photograph. Donning aqualungs, divers go out from the base to put in a working day at underwater projects.*

Where advanced fishing methods have been used, there is the danger of over-fishing. This implies the urgent need, before we go much further, in harvesting the living resources of the sea, to have a way of keeping a count of all the species we take from the sea so that we may be sure that they are renewed each year. Also, we must know how much we can increase the sustained yield when we begin to really farm the sea.

It is worthwhile to catalog some immediate and some distant exciting and potentially useful things we can do in and with the oceans. If some of these seem like irresponsible dreams, remember we live in days when purposeful dreaming becomes a reality so rapidly that it is almost regarded as respectable! If some seem like "stunts," it is worthwhile to remember that milestones of human achievement are necessary steps to give us the confidence to go on to even greater achievements and that yesterday's "stunts" are tomorrow's useful routines.

Remember, we are inventing the future, not merely predicting it. When people asked, "What will the new deep research submarines look for?", the best answer was: "For things we don't yet know." To survive in a new environment, true readiness is to be ready for the unexpected.

Let us start at the coastline. Instead of smoothing and concreting the coastlines, we may scallop them to build as many harbors and estuaries as we can and to lengthen the total coastline of the earth. There is a snowflake figure in mathematics which shows that any area, however small, can be enclosed by a line of infinite length. The smaller the scallops or harbors we build, the longer the coastline will be.

Next, perhaps we should heat some coastal waters not only so that we can swim in them, but also to make suitable warm water habitats for transplanting useful fish that previously could not multiply there. With the coming rash of large nuclear reactors, waste heat is regarded by the land engineer as a problem, because when it is introduced into cooling water it produces profound ecological effects. Many conventional conservationists consider any changes of this kind "bad." But if we go about it in a sound engineering way, we can introduce waste heat into the sea in a number of different ways and with beneficial effects to the ecology. Thereafter, this heat would no longer be waste but useful heat.

Because land engineering with its narrow focus of conserving our land and preventing it from being washed into the sea, and because of the almost total use and re-use of fresh water so that rivers will no longer flow into the sea, the sand that maintains beaches along the shorelines simply does not come down from the land. Beaches are not stationary. Sand is continually being taken away to accumulate in the canyons on the continental shelves or even in the deep sea. We'll need to dredge the sand back and remake the beaches. The beaches will still be in dynamic equilibrium but one link in the cycle will be provided by man's ocean engineering.

When we leave the shoreline, we will need vehicles to supplement the conventional ones which are so limited by wind and wave at the air-sea interface. We need increasingly to go down in submarines or up in *true* sea aircraft. Present seaplanes can make only emergency landings in the sea. We need the kind of sea aircraft that can fly out, settle, do its work in a high sea state, take off—vertically perhaps—and move on to the next job.

The present factory ships that catch and process whales and fish could grow into floating oceanic cities. We are beginning to get an idea of how to quiet waves by punching holes in harbor walls, much the same as we punch holes in acoustical tile to absorb sound energy. With these elements as a beginning, floating artificial harbors or wave-stemming walls of the floating cities would become possible. Or, more comfortable dwelling quarters could

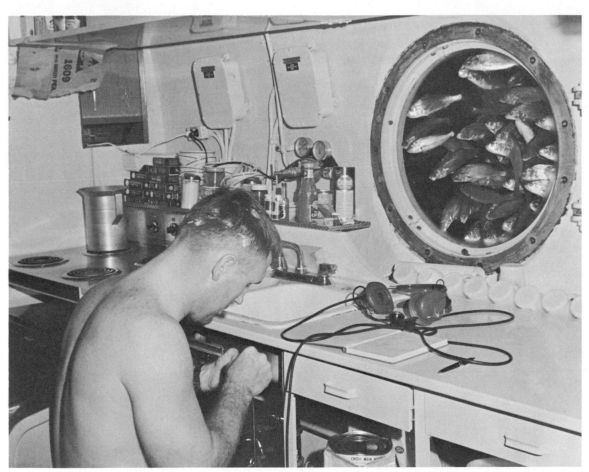

Fish look in through the window of Sealab II *two hundred feet down in the sea. The air pressure in the galley shown here is approximately seven times greater than at the surface and has severely dented the can of noodles at the bottom of the picture. Electrodes attached to the young diver's scalp permit measurement of important bodily functions under the severe conditions.*

92

This drawing of the author's conception of future underwater activities was first published in 1955. The underwater dwellings at the right have come true in the Sealab projects.

be stably floating a hundred feet or so below the surface where any wave motion is so damped out as to be unnoticeable. The artificial, harbors and other mother ship platforms could be arranged to retrieve small submersibles, to retrieve them *underwater,* so that a rendezvous in the high seas — a much more difficult job than a rendezvous in space — would become unnecessary.

After surface cities, habitations floating under the water, the step toward widespread structures on the bottom of the sea, would necessitate some ocean bottom engineering surveys. We will need to develop bottom vehicles to travel between the ocean cities. But even before this, we will have to develop a whole body of knowledge on submarine soil mechanics. How will the ocean sediments support foundations and crawling vehicles? How stable will the natural slopes be or the embankments we construct on the ocean bottom? How does the bottom erode?

How well will it hold moorings? We need an expedition across the bottom of the Atlantic and the Pacific in crawling, manned vehicles to survey the terrain — a Lewis and Clark trans-ocean bottom expedition. Until then, we will not know how currents, erosion and sediments will affect our engineering works. We do know from broken submarine cables that there are catastrophic phenomena much stronger than our concept of the "quiet of the deeps" would lead us to believe.

Also, before any widespread use of bottom structures, we need to study the properties of materials at very high pressures. Materials suffer effects at these pressures which are quite outside the domain of ordinary land engineering. Glass apparently becomes less brittle. The analytical mechanics of *thick* shell structures must be tackled without the simplifications which are satisfactory for the thin shells we use on land.

Already, thanks to the work of the physiologists, divers can live and work a few hundred feet down. There seems every prospect that a thousand feet is now not out of the question. Once people can work and live at a thousand feet, the whole of the continental shelf—an area of ten million square miles, larger than North America—will be opened up as a new continent for use. Oil drilling, mining, salvage and even fish farming can be done by people down there and not, as now, on the end of a string from a wobbly surface.

We are becoming accustomed to thinking that the potential of nuclear power is so great that we can dismiss other sources of power. The ocean holds great possibilities, too, but it is termed a "low grade" source because it will need to imprison, or otherwise use, a great deal of sea water to get a usable quantity of power. Therefore, the power of the sea has been regarded as a nuisance rather than a potential to be tapped. Usually when people think about the ocean's power, they think of tidal power. Indeed, there are several tidal power plants operating; in fact, tidal power was used to mill grain a century ago in Maine. But many times the tidal power potential exists in the difference in temperature between the top and the bottom of the ocean—the thermal gradient power. There are many places in the sea where differences of ten degrees occur over very short horizontal or vertical distances. So far there is only one small thermal gradient plant in operation.

With high structures at sea, wave power becomes a possibility. It is not easy to harness the up-and-down motion of the waves in any practical or efficient way when we have small objects bobbing on the surface even though the wave energy withstood by a ship's hull may be many times that required to propel the ship. But with the size of the structures we envisage, large artificial harbors and stable platforms, wave power becomes a possibility.

Ocean engineering in support of what we may call conventional fishing is already here. The behavioral scientists have a wealth of information on the response of fish to sonic, chemical and electronic stimuli that may take the place of ordinary bait. Floating chemical engineering factories can take the whole catch, sort the fish automatically—trash fish for meal, more valuable fish for canning or freezing and, more importantly, count the species to keep a check on what is the renewable harvest.

In gathering the living things of the ocean, ocean engineers should consider whether other living things themselves may do our building and collecting more efficiently than mechanical machines that we can devise. It would be very expensive to collect enough euphausid shrimp, but whales collect and convert them very efficiently. Perhaps we should be breeding whales instead of exterminating them. Can we accelerate the coral animal to build reefs? Can we use shellfish to concentrate minerals? Can we plant seaweed to stabilize beaches? Can we hybridize

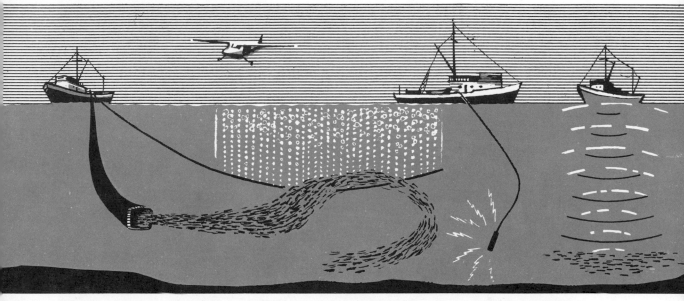

Modern apparatus has made new fishing methods possible. Fish can be spotted by aircraft or by a sonar device like that used by the vessel at right. Electric-shocking devices or bubble curtains can be used to herd the fish into a large suction funnel which can draw the fish directly into the hold of the fishing ship.

the plants that grow in sea water, the sea weeds, and use them much more extensively as sea fruits and vegetables? Perhaps we can even contribute to the land by using the wealth of information on halophytes —salty habitat plants—not only to grow useful food in sea or brackish water, but actually to desalinize water by the use of plants. Seaweed is a good source of iodine, for instance. Can we use plants to concentrate the salts we need?

These are the beginnings of farming the plants of the sea, but what about the animals? Plants are easier to farm and harvest because they may be rooted, but even if floating they are easy to control. Shellfish, which are indeed farmed, are the next easiest for the same reason. Oysters, clams and shrimp are cultured to a greater or lesser extent in ponds and semi-enclosed arms of the sea. Next, it is not much of a step to conceive of lobster traps on the bottom of the continental shelf acres in extent—in fact, bottom fish in general would seem to be most easily susceptible to fencing.

Then, how do we fertilize the sea? There are two ways in land farming, namely, plowing and adding nutrients. The counterpart of plowing in the sea is upwelling that brings nutrients from deeper water to the euphotic zone. Naturally, this is done by divergence or on a lee shore. The idea of doing this artificially by heating the ocean with a nuclear reactor at the bottom has been thought of, but on analysis does not seem economical. But the waste heat from nuclear reactors for other purposes may well be used in this way. The motions of the sea itself,

Porpoises will be the farmer's sheep dogs of the sea. In one of the projects performed from Sealab II, Tuffy, *the porpoise, carries messages from 200 feet down to the surface.*

which indeed cause upwelling, notably in such productive waters as the Humboldt Current, may be studied and ocean engineering may devise ways of making the sea plow itself more efficiently.

How can we fertilize the sea? It is impossible to add sufficient basic nutrients to open sea water, although this is possible in bay or pond water. In the sea these nutrients are stirred, mixed and diluted unlike fertilizers on land. It does seem possible, however, to add the trace substances, such as thiamine, once we know which are most important to growth. The study of trace elements, too, will lead us to more successful transplantation of useful fish from one area of the world to another. Then, too, by using what the marine scientists know about the food chain, we can eliminate some

of the unnecessary and less useful species, that is, intervene in a way that is essentially "weeding the sea."

One other aspect of the use of the sea, which is already with us and may grow even faster and stimulate ocean engineering more than these "more serious" uses of the sea, is the important part the sea can play in recreation in an increasingly crowded land world. Already you can purchase a small sporting submarine for not much more than the cost of an automobile. Thousands of people go down in the sea in aqualungs. Millions of dollars are spent on boats, elaborate fishing equipment and underwater cameras. Perhaps some of the first underwater structures will be for recreation. As mass-produced underwater vehicles come within the reach of many, underwater resorts will develop where people will drive their submobiles and visit reefs, watch the oceanic wild life in its natural habitat much the way we do in the wilderness and park areas on land.

These examples give you something of a vista of what ocean engineering can do in the sea. They show you how engineering and technology can bring everyone close to the oceans and can develop the sea's resources for everyone's use — just as on land, engineering has provided us with our dams, our fuels, our skyscrapers, highways, planes, ships, satellites; and the biological engineering which we call agriculture, has supplied us with our abundance of good food.

We need a way of bringing the vast body of scientific knowledge about the sea to the people who use it. We need to bring knowledge of the ocean to people other than the scientists who develop it, and not only to the engineers but to all related professions. We need an educational plan far broader than the existing ones that produce excellent marine scientists. There is not a single human activity that would not be affected by our Man-in-the-Sea program; and there is hardly any facet of man's knowledge and experience that will not be needed to complement this ocean engineering effort.

The artificial propagation of oysters for food is one of the world's oldest examples of seafarming. This oyster farm is in Tomales Bay, California.

The supplies of some minerals in the sea are considered inexhaustible. Nodules of Manganese show in this photograph of the ocean floor.

SEA GRANT COLLEGES

Just as the Land Grant Colleges were given grants of land in perpetuity for their experimental plots — in some cases lands in which mineral resources were found or that grew to be otherwise useful and served to provide income for the ongoing of the total enterprise — so Sea Grant Colleges should be given grants of seashore or lakeshore, seawater and bottom within territorial limits as their experimental plots to simulate the development of aquaculture in the waters and to exploit the natural resources of the sea bed. These watery grants would serve the additional purpose of preserving tracts of seashore and open waters from the fiercely competitive pressures of increasing population and industrialization — preserve them not only as natural habitats for ecological studies, but as important nursery areas for high sea fish and residences for inshore food fish and shell fish.

The Sea Grant Universities will benefit from Federal and State royalties from offshore leases — an incentive to further develop and exploit the sea.

We also will need county agents in hip boots — an aquacultural extension service of the Sea Grant College that takes the findings of the college or university onto the trawlers, drilling rigs, merchant ships, and down to the submotels. We will need sea home economics, too. Even if we had abundant protein from the sea today, a selling job would need to be done to remove taste prejudices and taboos, and this could be done

by such a down-to-earth service, yet one which touches more people than the erudite things we do in universities — home economics.

As we breed and farm fish, we will need to have fish pathologists, experts on the diseases and parasites that may plague our flocks in the sea or our plants. We will no longer be able to tolerate epidemics like the blooming of a red tide of dynoflaggellates that cause widespread fish kills and are concentrated by mollusks poisonous to people.

Law is an utterly important adjunct to any widespread exploitation of the sea. We need clarification of the law of the sea and a way of, on one hand, being able to grant rights so that a group investing capital in vast projects may be assured of some stability toward a reasonable return and, on the other hand, better legal controls to prevent overfishing.

Public administration, with due regard to national and international politics, must find a way out of the dilemma that is posed when nobody owns what's in the sea, nobody feels responsible for its controlled exploitation.

But to do all those things we need Sea Grant Universities and Colleges committed to the mastery, exploitation and preservation of the sea. Just as the scholars in the Land Grant Colleges developed a passion for benefiting and preserving the land, we must seek, through a welding together of science, art, literature, engineering, medicine, law, public administration and politics, to de-

99

velop a public which will not only homestead our new spaces in the sea but colonize and civilize them.

The marine engineer who emerges from our Sea Grant institutions will be as different from the old-fashioned marine engineer as the satellite engineer is from the one who operates a heating plant. The aquaculturist will be just as different from the conventional fisherman. Oceanic engineering and aquaculture—the control of the sea for man's purposes —present a magnificent challenge to our imagination and inventiveness. The National Sea Grant College Act, proposed by the author in 1963, was signed by President Lyndon B. Johnson on October 15, 1966 to provide a framework for the United States to develop the bounty of the seas for the benefit of all people.

The oceans represent military, recreational, economic, artistic and intellectual outlets of unlimited scope. Thus they can offer us more space in which to remain human. The sea—beautiful and dangerous, elegant and strong, bountiful and whimsical—not only challenges us but offers to every "man in the street" the exciting participation of being a "man in the sea." Like a military operation where a war is not won until the area is occupied, we will master the sea only when we occupy it.

Marine engineers collecting sand dollars for a geology laboratory specimen collection.

The challenge and bounties of the seas await those with imagination, curiosity, and inventiveness.

Glossary of Terms

Abyss: A deep zone in the ocean extending from about 300 fathoms to the sea floor, an area without light and near freezing temperatures.

Age of water: The time elapsed since a water mass was last at the surface and in contact with the atmosphere. The water's age gives an indication of the rate of overturn of ocean water, an important factor in the use of the oceans for dumping radioactive wastes and determining the rate of replenishment of nutrients.

Algae: The simple forms of green plants possessing chlorophyll; includes diatoms and seaweeds.

Amphibious landing craft: Vehicles that can navigate on both the sea and dry land.

Anadromous: A form of life cycle among fishes which mature in the ocean, and the adults ascend streams and rivers to spawn in fresh water.

Aquaculture: The science of underwater farming and development of new sea foods.

Atmosphere: The amount of pressure exerted by air on water and all objects on this planet. One atmosphere amounts to a pressure of 14.7 pounds per square inch. For each 33 feet of depth in the water, the pressure increases by one atmosphere.

Ballast: Weights carried by a submarine, ship or balloon that can be released to cause the vessel to float upwards by its increased buoyancy.

Barometer: An instrument for measuring atmospheric pressure.

Bathymetric charts: Charts showing contours of the sea bottom much like contour maps on land.

Bathyscaph: A free, manned deep diving vehicle used for exploring the deep ocean.

Bathythermograph: An instrument for obtaining a record of temperature against depth in the ocean, trailed by a cable from a ship underway.

Benthos: Bottom dwelling forms of marine life.

Calving (of icebergs): When a mass of ice breaks off from its parent glacier and falls into the sea, we say an iceberg has been calved.

Challenger deep: A 35,800-foot-deep trench near Guam in the Pacific Ocean. The bottom of this trench is the deepest known place on earth. The bathyscaph *Trieste* descended to its bottom in 1960.

Challenger Expedition: The first extensive oceanographic research expedition from 1872 to 1876 by the British in the *H.M.S. Challenger*.

Continental Shelves: An underwater plain bordering nearly every continent which gradually slopes downward to a depth of about 600 feet and then plunges more steeply to the ocean depths.

Corers: Tubes that are driven or forced in the ocean bottom to take sediment samples.

Coriolis force: An object moving over the earth's surface tends to move in a straight line in space. But the earth's surface moves under the object. It therefore seems to us that the moving object curves to the right in the Northern Hemisphere and to the left in the Southern Hemisphere. The Coriolis force is an imaginary aid that helps us to work out such problems on our rotating earth. The force is considered to act at right angles to the movement of the object.

Diatom: A microscopic phytoplankton organism. Diatoms are one of the most abundant primary food sources of marine animals.

Echo sounding: Determining the depth of water by measuring the time interval between emission of a sonic or ultrasonic signal and the return of its echo from the bottom.

Electromagentic spectrum: Consists of all wavelengths of radiation from the longest through the shortest, including radio waves, ultra high frequency waves, microwaves, infrared waves, visible light, ultraviolet waves, X-rays, and gamma rays.

Electrode: The terminal of a source of electricity. There generally are two electrodes: a positive anode and a negative cathode.

Elliptical: An ellipse is a flattened circle with one diameter greater than the other; all closed orbits in space are elliptical.

Escapement clock: An escapement regulates a clock to keep time by the oscillations of a balance wheel or pendulum.

Extraterrestrial body: The moon, meteorites or other objects in space away from the earth.

Fathom: The common nautical unit of measure used in all depth measurements. One fathom is equal to 6 feet.

Gamma: The name given to radiation, much like X-rays, but much shorter in wave length; radioactive elements give off gamma rays and natural cosmic rays contain gamma rays.

Geophysics: The physics on nature of the earth. It deals with the composition and physical phenomena of the earth, sea, and air; it includes the study of terrestrial magnetism, atmospheric electricity, gravity, seismology, volcanology, oceanography, meteorology, and related sciences.

Hydrography: That science which deals with the measurement and descriptions of the physical features of the oceans, seas, lakes, rivers and coastal areas, as to their use for navigational purposes.

Ion: An atom or group of atoms that has either a positive or negative electrical charge. The dissolved salts in seawater are ions. The process that takes place when ions form is called *ionization.*

Ionosphere: That part of the atmosphere 50 miles above the earth's surface which contains ions. The ionosphere reflects long radio waves back to the ground.

Knot: A unit of speed of one nautical mile (6,076.12 feet) per hour. If a ship travels ten nautical miles per hour, her speed is ten knots.

Latitude: A term describing a given location as so many degrees north or south of the equator. The equator is designated as 0°.

Longitude: A term describing the number of degrees east or west of a line drawn from the North Pole down through Greenwich, England to the South Pole. This line being 0° runs through the Eastern Hemisphere and is called the Prime meridian.

Mantle: The relatively plastic region between the crust and the core of the earth.

Marine Biology: The study of plants and animals living in the sea.

Marine chronometer: An extremely accurate escapement clock regulated by a balance wheel which measures time accurately enough to tell longitude from the sun or stars.

Mean sea level: Tides, waves and currents change the sea level from time to time and place to place so scientists use an average or mean sea level from which to measure heights above ground and depths of the ocean.

Oceanography: The study of the sea, embracing all knowledge pertaining to the sea's physical boundaries, the chemistry and physics of sea water, and marine biology.

Photosynthesis: Literally assembling with light; the green pigment, chlorophyll, absorbs light and combines it with inorganic chemicals to make food.

Phytoplankton: The minute green plants that grow at the surface of the sea and where sunshine reaches them; the grasses of the sea.

Pockmarked: Pitted or cratered like the surface of the moon.

Protoplanet: The original or beginning of our planet.

Radioisotope atomic power: Radioactive materials give out radiation which can be used to generate electricity or make steam, etc., as they decay.

Salinity: A measure of the total degree of saltiness of sea water.

Seamount: Underwater mountains that rise up steeply from the floor of the ocean.

Seawater: The water of the seas differs from fresh water by its salinity. The amount of salinity greatly affects its physical characteristics.

Seawater batteries: Silver-zinc batteries which are activated by the flow of sea water through them.

Seismograph: An instrument used to measure and record earthquake vibrations and other earth tremors.

Shoals: Shallow parts of the sea which may be dangerous to ships and may even be exposed above water at low tide.

Subsurface rivers: Under many of the surface ocean currents are deep currents often going in a different direction; these may be called subsurface rivers.

Telemeter: To measure at a distance; as, for instance, measuring the temperature of the high atmosphere from a balloon carrying a thermometer which radios back its measurements.

Thermal gradient power: The difference in temperature between the warm surface water and the cold bottom water which can be used to run a heat engine; water or some other liquid can be boiled under vacuum or suitable pressure at the surface, the vapor used to drive a turbine and then condensed in the cold water at the bottom to repeat the cycle.

Thermocline: A zone of rapid temperature changes lying between the rapidly warmed surface currents and the cold water of the subsurface rivers. Fishes cannot cross this invisible "barrier."

Tide: The periodic rising and falling of the earth's oceans and atmosphere. It is the result of the forces of the moon and sun acting upon the rotating earth.

Trawls: Cone or funnel shaped nets dragged along the bottom of the sea to trap fish in; hence, fishing boats are called trawlers.

Twilight zone: A submarine zone, extending from about 100 fathoms to 250 fathoms in depth. It lies between the surface lighted zone and the deeper abyss which is without light.

Index

sea for, 96-97
"Red tide," 63,99
Reptiles, 54
Research ships, 21,22-25,26,27, 32,40,55. *See also* Diving craft
Resorts, underwater, 96-97
Reversing thermometers, 29
Rhode Island School of Oceanography, 4
Richardson, Jonathan, 6
Right whales, 59
"River in the sea," 46
Rivers, subsurface, 36,46,105
Ross, Sir James, 32

S

Salinity, of sea water, 24,28, 29-30,39,42,49,61,104
Salmon, 66
Salt. *See* Salinity
Salvage, 94
Sampling net, 27
San Diego, Calif., 41
Sand, 61,66,91
Sand dollars, 54,100
Sargasso Sea, 29
Satellite engineer, 100
Satellites, 19,42,66,97
Scalloping the coastline, 91
Scotia Sea, 55
Scripps Institute of Oceanography, 4
Scuba, 10
Sea. *See* Oceans
Sea aircraft, 92
Sea cucumbers, 54
Sea home economics, 99
Sea level, 28-29,104
Sea monsters, 21
"Sea smoke," 10
Sea spiders, 55
Sea urchins, 54
Sea walls, 62
Sea water, *defined*, 104
Sea-grant colleges, 99
"Sealab" projects, 71,90,92,93, 96
Sealab II, 90,92,93,96
Seals, 56,57,59
Seamounts, 14,16,32,36,39,104
Seaplanes, 92
Seashore, 61-62,69,99
Seawater batteries, 104
Seaweed, 94-95,102
Sediments, 9,32,33,54,61,93
Seismographs, 32,104
Self-contained Underwater Breathing Apparatus (Scuba), 10
Senate, U.S., 45
Shellfish, 22,54,63,88,94,95,99
Ships, oceanographic research, 21,22-25,26,27,32,40,55. *See also* Diving craft
Shoals, 104
Shrimp, 53,60,94,95
Shrimp boat, 60
Shrimp net, 60
Siberia, 15

Siebe, August, 70
Sierra Club, 4
Skin diving, 67, 71
Smithsonian Institution, 4
Snails, 58
Snares Island penguins, 56
Soil mechanics, submarine, 93
Sonar, 21,31
Sound energy, 92
Sound forecasting, 49
Sound rays, 34
Sound transmission, 34,49
Sound waves, 49
Soundings, 32,34,49,55,103
South Orkney Island, 55
South Pole, 20
Southern Hemisphere, 12,103
Space science, 83
Spilhaus, Athelstan, 6,30,45
Sport fishermen, 67
Sporting submarine, 96
Springs, fresh water, in the ocean, 88
Squid, 21
Star I, 81
Star II, 78,79,80,81
Star III, 80,81
Starfishes, 54
Stirring, of the ocean, 49,66
Submarine beacons, 36
Submarine warfare, 34
Submarines, 10,31,34,35,41,49, 78,92,96
  nuclear, 10,31,35
  sporting, 96
Submobiles, 97
Submotels, 99
Subsurface rivers, 36,46,105
Surf, 46
Swell, 46

T

Tagging, of fish, 66
Te Vega, 21
Telemeters, 45, 105
Television, 31,32,68,77
Television aquariums, 68
Temperature, of ocean waters, 28,29,30,34,39,42,49
Thermal gradient power, 94,105
Thermocline, 105
Thermometers, 28,29,105
Thermostats, 33
Thiamine, 96
Thompson, Charles Wyville, 22,24
Tide predictor, 47
Tides, 28,34,46,47,53,105
Time problems in navigation, 19-20
Titanic, 48
Tomales Bay, Calif., 97
Tracers, radioactive, 29
Trawlers, 60,99,105
Trawls, 22,30,60,78,105
Trenches, underwater, 16,73, 102
Trieste I, 73,80,81,102
Trieste II, 74,80,81
Trilobites, 54

Tristan da Cunha Islands, 69
Tropical tuna, 59
Tuffy, the porpoise, 96
Tuna fishing, 49,59,66
Twilight zone, 105

U

Ultraviolet light, 54,103
Undersea fresh water springs, 88
Underwater cameras, 32,55,96
Underwater communications, 43
Underwater landslides, 83
Underwater resorts, 96-97
Uninhabited islands, 69
University of Miami, 4
Upwellings, 49,95-96
U.S.S. *Perch*, 31

V

Vema, 25,26
Volcanic springs, 14

W

Walruses, 56,57
Walsh, Lt. Don, 73
Waste, radioactive, 64,65,102
Waste heat, uses for, 66,91,95
Water:
  age of, 102
  bottom water, 29
  density of, 28,29
  depth measurements, 32,34, 42,49,55,103
  desalination, 56,95
  fresh, needs for, 61
  types, 28
Water divining, in the sea, 88
Water samplers, 28,30
Water waves, theory of, 36,37
Wave energy, 45
Waves, 28,36,37,45,46,49,62, 83,88,89,92,94
  forecasts of, 46,49
  internal, 28
  patterns of, 37
  power from, 94
  quieting, 92
  theory of water waves, 36,37
  white-caps, 36
Weather predictions, 29,43,46, 49
"Weeding the sea," 96
Whales, 10,52,53,55,56,59,66, 92,94
White-caps, 36
Wilderness, ocean, 69
Winch, 28,32
Wind, 10,34,36,46,49,62,89,92
Wind divergence, 49
Woods Hole Oceanographic Institution, 4,24,42,77
World War I, 34
World War II, 6,34

X

X-rays, 27,103

Z

Zooplankton, 55

109

Picture Credits

All original art work was prepared for Creative Educational Society by Bueford D. Smith.

American Geographical Society and Athelstan Spilhaus: 15 (right), 29

American Museum of Natural History: 56

Beach Erosion Board and Pacific Air Industries: 62

Bolin, R.: 21 (lower)

ESSA: 21 (upper)

Food and Agriculture Organization, United Nations: 50

Galloway, Ewing: 8, 105

General Dynamics Corporation: 10 (upper right), 43, 77 (lower right), 78, 79, 84, 85

Harmon Foundation, New York: 18

Interagency Committee on Oceanography and Dr. Richard B. Terry: 74 (lower), 76 (lower)

Maxwell, C. G.: 69, 101

Naval Electronics Laboratory: 39, 74 (upper)

Ocean Systems, Inc.: 82 (lower), 83

Office of Naval Research: 77 (upper right)

Perry Submarine Builders, Inc.: 82 (upper)

Reynolds Submarine Services Corporation: 86

Rockefeller Foundation: 68

Ryther: 98

Scripps Institution of Oceanography: 9, 37, 41 (upper and lower), 52, 53

Smith, Bueford D.: Cover

Smithsonian Institution: 10 (lower), 24, 25, 26, 27 (upper & lower), 32, 33, 40 (upper and lower), 54, 60 (lower), 64, 67, 75, 97

Socony Mobile Oil Company, Inc.: 100

Spilhaus, Athelstan: 12, 13, 14, 15 (left), 16, 22, 23, 36, 42 (lower left), 44, 70, 72, 73 (lower right), 93, 95

U. S. Coast and Geodetic Survey: 46 (left and right), 47, 48

U. S. Fish and Wildlife Service: 20, 49, 57, 58, 59, 60 (upper)

U. S. Hydrographic Office: 28, 30, 38

U. S. Naval Ordinance Test Station: 87

U. S. Navy: 10 (upper left), 31 (upper and lower), 35, 55, 71, 73 (upper), 90, 92, 96

Westinghouse Electric Corporation, Underseas Division: 76 (upper), 88, 89

Woods Hole Oceanographic Institution: 42 (right), 77 (upper left)